Container Gardening *for* Canada

Laura Peters • Alison Beck • Don Williamson

LONE PINE

Lone Pine Publishing

The Publisher: Lone Pine Publishing
10145 – 81 Avenue
Edmonton, AB, T6E 1W9 Canada
Website: www.lonepinepublishing.com

Library and Archives Canada Cataloguing in Publication

Peters, Laura, 1968-
    Container gardening for Canada / Laura Peters, Alison Beck, Don Williamson.

Includes index.
ISBN-13: 978-1-55105-588-6

    1. Container gardening--Canada. I. Beck, Alison, 1971-
II. Williamson, Don, 1962- III. Title.

SB418.P48 2007   635.9'860971   C2006-906302-8

Editorial Director: Nancy Foulds
Project Editor: Sheila Quinlan
Editors: Sheila Quinlan, Carol Woo
Photo Coordinator: Don Williamson
Production Manager: Gene Longson
Book Design & Layout: Heather Markham
Cover Design: Gerry Dotto
Production Support: Willa Kung, Trina Koscielnuk

Front cover photograph by Proven Winners

All photos by Laura Peters except:
Sandra Bit 24b, 51a, 151b; Conard-Pyle Roses 181b; Tamara Eder 21b, 55a&b, 56b, 65, 78, 91a, 99b, 100, 105a&b, 118a&b, 130a, 132a&b, 140a, 141, 152b, 160b, 161, 164, 179, 182a&b, 186b, 192, 194, 209a; Jen Fafard 37b, 205b; Derek Fell 88, 129, 135; Erika Flatt 42, 87; Saxon Holt 74, 146; Dawn Loewen 156b; Janet Loughrey 126, 187; Heather Markham 136; Tim Matheson 38a&b, 54a, 63, 64a&b, 67a, 79b, 92, 108, 109, 115b&c, 134b, 142, 152a, 160a&c, 167, 172b, 191, 193a&b, 197, 204, 208; Kim O'Leary 91b, 124; Allison Penko 82, 99a, 104, 140b, 148, 149b, 150, 156a, 205a; Photos. com 54b, 202; Proven Winners 11,16a,17a, 18b&c, 19b, 21a, 22a&b, 36b, 37a, 52b, 53a, 57a, 60a&b, 61, 62, 66, 68, 72, 77, 95a, 96a, 97a, 98, 101, 110a&b, 112a, 114, 117, 121a, 127, 133, 137, 143, 154, 163, 166, 169, 170, 174, 175, 180, 184, 185, 188, 189a, 198, 199, 201b, 203, 207; Robert Ritchie 56a; Nanette Samol 25a, 26b, 27a,c&d, 31c, 40, 41a&b, 43a&b, 44a,b&c, 45a,b,c&d, 47a, 48b, 59a&b; Peter Thompstone 162; Tim Wood 67b, 111a,b&c, 115a, 119, 130b, 149a, 157a&b, 209b.

This book is not intended as a 'how-to' guide for eating garden plants. No plant or plant extract should be consumed unless you are certain of its identity and toxicity and of your potential for allergic reactions.

We acknowledge the financial support of the Government of Canada through the Book Publishing Industry Development Program (BPIDP) for our publishing activities.

PC:*P14*

Table of Contents

Preface

Container gardening is nothing new, but it has changed over the years—dramatically in some areas, but slowly evolving with gardening trends and traditions in others.

Most gardeners are familiar with the common, reliable plants within their region. This familiarity also applies to arranging the plants in the same configuration year after year. We've all seen or planted a dracaena spike in the centre of a container, surrounded by red geraniums and trailing lobelia, then edged in bright white alyssum. There is nothing wrong with this traditional arrangement, but nowadays endless possibilities exist for plant combinations in containers. Regardless of what zone you're in, from coast to coast and for every level of gardening expertise, there are new and exciting ways to garden in containers. You have only to use your imagination, open your mind to new plant combination possibilities and look at container gardening from a whole new perspective.

Most gardeners in zones with short growing seasons and very cold winters shy away from using hardy plants in their containers for fear of losing them over winter. This possibility in most cases won't happen if a few basic needs are met. Plants may become damaged or die during winter, but that's okay—let go of your emotional or monetary attachment to your plants, at least to a certain extent, and don't hold back from expressing your true gardening artistry. So what if you plant a perennial in a container, attempt to overwinter it and it dies. If you know that it may die, then you'll be less disappointed and maybe will have discovered the new appeal and versatility of your containers, awoken a desire to try something new and found a need to experiment further.

Gardening in containers offers a unique opportunity to experiment with an amazing selection of plants available throughout Canada, including tropicals, woody ornamentals, annuals, perennials, herbs, vines and everything in between. There's a whole new world of inspiring and endless designs and combinations based on colour, style, impact and form. Be brave, try something new and mix it up; never settle for the same old humdrum annual arrangement. Plant your vegetables with your annuals and your perennials with your vines. Combine shrubs with tropicals. Switch it up again every opportunity that you get, from one season to the next and from year to year. Don't let the opportunity to explore and get dirty pass you by. All the best.

~Laura Peters

The Plants at a Glance

Pictorial Guide in Alphabetical Order

Aeonium
p. 62

African Lily
p. 63

Angel's Trumpet
p. 65

Arborvitae
p. 66

Argyranthemum
p. 68

Asparagus Fern
p. 69

Athyrium
p. 70

Basil
p. 73

Bay Laurel
p. 74

Bacopa
p. 72

Begonia
p. 75

Bidens
p. 77

Black-Eyed Susan
p. 78

Black-Eyed Susan Vine
p. 80

Blood Grass
p. 81

Blue Oat Grass
p. 82

Bougainvillea
p. 83

Bugleweed
p. 84

Calla Lily
p. 85

Catch-Fly
p. 88

Cilantro • Coriander
p. 89

Canna Lily
p. 87

Clematis
p. 90

Cleome
p. 92

Clover
p. 93

Coleus
p. 94

Coral Bells
p. 96

Cranesbill
p. 98

Cuphea
p. 101

Dahlia
p. 102

Daylily
p. 104

Crocosmia
p. 100

Dogwood
p. 106

Dwarf Morning Glory
p. 109

Elder
p. 110

Elephant Ears
p. 112

Dusty Miller
p. 108

English Ivy
p. 113

Euonymus
p. 114

Fan Flower
p. 116

Fescue
p. 117

Flowering Maple
p. 118

Fothergilla
p. 119

Fountain Grass
p. 120

Geranium
p. 122

Hakone Grass
p. 125

Hebe
p. 126

Heliotrope
p. 127

Glory Bush
p. 124

Hens and Chicks
p. 128

Holly
p. 129

Hosta
p. 131

Hyssop
p. 135

Impatiens
p. 136

Ipomoea
p. 137

Hydrangea
p. 133

Iris
p. 139

Kalanchoe
p. 141

Lady's Mantle
p. 142

Lamium
p. 143

Lavender
p. 145

Licorice Plant
p. 147

Lilac
p. 148

Lilyturf
p. 150

Leymus
p. 146

Lotus Vine
p. 153

Lungwort
p. 154

Lobelia
p. 151

Magnolia
p. 156

Maidenhair Fern
p. 158

Lysimachia
p. 155

Maple
p. 159

Marguerite Daisy
p. 161

Million Bells
p. 162

Mondo Grass
p. 163

Monkey Flower
p. 164

Nasturtium
p. 165

Nemesia
p. 166

Nicotiana
p. 167

Oregano
p. 168

Osteospermum
p. 169

Oxalis
p. 170

Pansy
p. 171

Parsley
p. 173

Perilla
p. 175

Persicaria
p. 176

Penstemon
p. 174

Petunia
p. 177

Piggyback Plant
p. 179

Plectranthus
p. 180

Rose
p. 181

Phormium
p. 178

Rosemary
p. 183

Salvia
p. 185

Scarlet Runner Bean
p. 187

Sedge
p. 188

Rush
p. 184

Sedum
p. 190

Serviceberry
p. 191

Snapdragon
p. 192

Snow-in-Summer
p. 194

Spider Plant
p. 195

Spruce
p. 196

Spurge
p. 197

Swan River Daisy
p. 198

Sweet Flag
p. 199

Thyme
p. 200

Tradescantia
p. 201

Tulip
p. 202

Verbena
p. 203

Viburnum
p. 204

Vinca
p. 206

Weigela
p. 207

Yarrow
p. 208

Yew
p. 209

Yucca
p. 210

Introduction

Container gardening is one of the most practical and flexible forms of gardening and is suitable for every level of gardening expertise, demographic and space available within a landscape, even if that landscape is only a balcony. Almost every plant that can be grown in a conventional garden can be grown on a smaller scale in a container. Container gardening is an excellent opportunity for gardeners who live in apartments, condominiums or small homes with only a patio or balcony on which to grow and nurture their own gardens. Gardeners can use containers to create theme gardens, grow vegetables, plant an orchard, pick flowers for a vase or add fresh herbs to favourite recipes. A small deck or patio can be transformed into a tropical oasis, an English cottage garden or a shaded woodland when pots of different shapes and sizes are filled with varied plant combinations to achieve a certain feel, look or environment. Even one large container can provide you with all the pleasure gardening has to offer.

Container gardening is also a benefit to people with limited mobility, such as the disabled and the elderly, who require easy accessibility to their gardens. A garden with wide paths, raised beds and containers is ideal for able-bodied gardeners but even better for those who require the extra space for accessibility and stability. A stable, wide edge of a raised bed offers a seating area at a comfortable height for people who cannot work for extended periods while standing.

Container gardening is also a wonderful way to enhance larger gardens and landscapes. Containers expand the space available for growing plants, especially those plants that require specific growing conditions, such as poor soil or a soil that is not typical for the area. Many containers can be easily moved to take advantage of light conditions not available in the regular planting areas of your garden or landscape, and containers with more tender plants can be moved to areas where they can be protected from the elements. Container plants are used as focal points, set in places to draw your attention or to mark entrances such as doorways, sidewalks, driveways and garden paths. Beautifully planted containers can also be used to draw your eyes away from distracting items or areas you would prefer to remain unnoticed.

Containers can be used to provide seasonal displays throughout the year, depending on the region. Containers can also be placed in beds and borders to fill gaps left by plants that finished blooming earlier in the season or were decimated by pests or disease, or by plants that were simply not performing as desired. Using containers as a physical barrier to confine plants with an invasive tendency will allow you to grow these plants without having to contend with their spreading into unwanted places.

Containers are also great places to experiment with companion planting: plants that form a symbiotic relationship when planted together. For example, one plant provides protection from pests while another plant provides it with nutrients. Overall, this combination of plants may also improve the growing conditions by shading the roots or suppressing weed growth.

Container gardening can be a time and money saver. Many of the tedious chores like weeding, lawn mowing, digging and raking are reduced or eliminated when you garden in containers. The use of automated watering systems or water-holding polymers and other materials, combined with slow-release fertilizers, can make your container garden a very low-maintenance affair. The smaller gardening area will also cost less than an average garden. You will have to make an initial investment in containers and a few tools and supplies to get started, but your annual costs will include only plants, fertilizer and growing media. Once you become more proficient at growing plants in containers, you'll learn how to cut costs even further, as well as the overall amount of work involved.

The only limits to what can be done with container gardening are the limits you place on yourself. Just let your imagination run wild, and remember that making mistakes is all part of the learning process. There is really no way to fail at gardening if you keep an open mind and just have fun experimenting. That's the beauty of container gardening—there's no long-term commitment. You can change your containers completely from one season to the next, regardless of what you've chosen to grow.

A well-designed container provides interest in the garden (left). Group plants with the same needs together (above).

Container Design

A well-designed container or grouping of containers can look stunning with trailing plants cascading over the edges, colourful mounds of delicate flowers and interesting foliage filling the centres. Container gardening will allow you the opportunity to create any style possible to suit the container's setting, whether it's traditional, eclectic, contemporary or industrial. This form of gardening also appeals to those who enjoy experimenting with combinations of plants until they discover the perfect arrangement, and even to those who prefer to switch it up from year to year, following the trends. Gardening in all its incarnations should be fun and enjoyable, and container gardening is no exception.

Choosing what you like from what will grow well in the conditions of your growing space is one of the steps to planning any garden. Deciding how to combine these plants is another important step. Containers should be treated like small flowerbeds, and the same principles of design apply as with ground-based plantings. There are no hard and fast rules to container design, but the following suggestions may help to determine what will grow successfully in combinations and what will appeal to the eye. Just remember that everyone is different, and what appeals to one person visually may not appeal to another. This is an opportunity for you to indulge yourself and make your own design choices.

You should try to group plants that have the same needs together, such as water-loving plants, shade-tolerant plants or drought-resistant plants. This will make it simpler to take care of each container and can help to prevent problems with insects and diseases.

If you are combining several different types of plants in one container, generally keep the tallest ones in the middle or, if the container will be against a wall, fence or railing, to the back of the container. Compact and trailing plants can be kept closer to the front or the edges of the container so that they are not lost visually. Some of the more robust trailing plants are good choices for the corners of square containers, where they have some extra room to spread. Careful planning allows for the best light to reach all plants, makes them all easy to see and enjoy and gives the containers an attractive, well-balanced appearance.

Combining several different types of plants together (above & below).

You can use tall, sun-loving plants to provide shade for other plants. A trellis covered with tall, fast-growing morning glories, scarlet runner beans or hops will shade containers of impatiens or hostas.

There are other features you may want consider when planning your containers. You can choose plants that all flower at the same time, or whose flowering times are staggered. Flower and foliage colour are important considerations, as is the texture of the plants. Combining different features creates interest and contrast in your containers. Other design elements to be aware of include scale and proportion, shape, balance and repetition.

PROVEN WINNERS

Cool colours (above) are soothing. Colour echoing with warm colours (below).

Colour

We tend to focus on colour because it is often the first thing we notice in a garden. The difference between a container garden and one grown in the ground is the area of display. A container garden is confined and right in front of you, while in a more traditional ground-based garden, it takes more effort to make a dramatic effect with colour.

Sometimes knowing where to start is overwhelming. Take inspiration from home decorating and lifestyle magazines or anything that inspires you. Keep in mind that different colours have different effects on our senses. Cool colours, such as blue, purple and green, are soothing and can make small spaces seem bigger. Warm colours, such as red, orange and yellow, are more stimulating and appear to fill large spaces. White combines well with any colour, and plants that bloom in white help to keep the garden from becoming a blurry, tangled mess.

People use colour in their interior spaces to relax when at home. This formula can also be used outdoors, especially in small spaces. Green combinations can provide a refreshing feel to a space, while pinks and blues can invoke a romantic environment. Fiery yellows, oranges and reds will add a liveliness and warmth to even the largest, most imposing spaces, and bronze, brown and neutral tones can appear contemporary and classy.

There are a couple of aspects of colour to be aware of when planning your containers: colour echoing and colour harmonies.

Colour echoing uses one colour, which can be of various hues and intensities, repeated throughout the garden to produce unity and flow. This has the effect of making it easy for your eyes to flow from one part of the garden to the next without abrupt changes. It is wise to keep the colour of your house, out-buildings and structures such as fences in mind when deciding what colour or colours to use.

Colour harmonies involve the colour designs we use to plan our containers, and they are easy to understand with the use of a colour wheel.

Monochromatic designs use one colour that varies in hue and intensity, or colours very close to it on the colour wheel. For example, a monochromatic planting of yellow may include something very close to it on the colour wheel, such as including yellow-green part of the wheel, without disturbing the harmony of the planting.

Using black and white in the garden.

PROVEN WINNERS

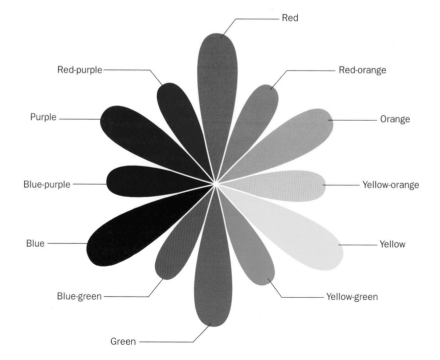

Red

Red-purple

Red-orange

Purple

Orange

Blue-purple

Yellow-orange

Blue

Yellow

Blue-green

Yellow-green

Green

Monochromatic (above). Complimentary (below).   Analogous (above). Polychromatic (below).

Analogous colour designs use colours that are next to each other on the wheel, such as using blues with violets and greens. These colours add a little more spice to a design while maintaining the same mood of the planting.

Complementary colour designs use colours that are opposite to each other on the colour wheel. These combinations make bold and dramatic plantings that are hard not to notice.

There are now a number of plants available that come in very dark shades very close to black. The use of black, white and grey colours in planting designs can help make other colours really stand out, add depth to smaller areas and plantings and help to tone down strong and complementary colours. A planting with all white flowers is a good choice for those whose gardening time is limited to twilight and evening hours.

Polychromatic colour designs are those that most closely resemble the designs found in nature—a mixture of colours seemingly tossed together in a haphazard manner. These can be some of the easiest designs to do.

Texture

Texture is an important consideration in container planting, as different plant textures affect the perception of garden size and space. Integrating textural foliage into a container design encourages people to get up close to touch the leaves and flowers. You'll want to determine whether foliage is rough, soft, spiky or smooth. Small leaves, or those that that are finely divided, are considered finely textured and create a sense of greater space and light, while larger leaves are often considered coarsely textured and can be seen easily from a distance. Some gardens have been designed solely on the basis of texture.

Foliage is the most important plant feature for achieving different textures in a planting. Textures, colours and the size of the foliage can vary greatly, creating a myriad of combinations. Flowers come and go, but a container garden planned with careful attention to foliage, using a mix of coarse, medium and fine textures will always be interesting.

Scale and Proportion

The scale and proportion of plants should match the size of the containers you plan to use. Larger containers can look equally stunning with one solitary plant as a magnificent or simple specimen as they do with a large number of plants. Smaller containers aren't much different, as long as the space allotted is appropriate for the plants chosen. For standard container designs featuring a tall focal plant, the finished height should ideally be one to one-and-a-half times the height of the container, and the planting should be roughly triangular in form. This is not a hard and fast rule but a flexible guideline to be adapted according to the shape of the container. The exception would be with large specimen plants, which demand their own container, or at most have a fringe of trailing plants, and often exceed the suggested plant-to-container height ratio.

The scale and proportion of the containers and plants should complement their surroundings. Often one large,

The scale and proportion of your containers should match their surroundings.

A tall structural plant in a very tall container adds drama to a front yard.

well-planted container will look better in a smaller location than in an array of smaller containers. Window boxes should match the style of the structure and enhance the space from both inside and outside the window. Too much height will block sunlight from the house, but some height in the middle of the box can be a nice touch.

Shape

It is important to choose plants with different shapes to provide variety in your container plantings. The careful use of shape can help to add drama and emotion or tranquility and peacefulness. Imagine the silhouette of a city skyline and how dull it would look if all the buildings were square blocks of the same size. Tall, structural plants can be effective on their own, but they also work well as the main feature within a mixed arrangement. Rounded, billowy

plants add bulk to a container planting. Short, trailing or mat-forming plants can soften the edges of containers and add depth, as the plants effectively increase the diameter of the container. Short, upright plants are great for filling open spots. Do not forget the shapes of the containers themselves. Matching the shapes of your containers with your garden location can create stunning results.

Balance

Balance is easy to visualize by thinking of a scale, where what is on one side must balance with what is on the other side. In a design, balanced plantings are pleasing to the eye. There is symmetrical balance, such as one would see in a formal garden where a line can be drawn up the centre and one side is the mirror of the other, and asymmetrical balance, where the two sides are not the same but have the same visual effect. An example

focal point with arms radiating out in all directions. Radial symmetry is achieved when all arms are balanced.

Repetition

Repetition can be used in areas where you want to bring symmetry into play. Repeating patterns is a design element that is fundamental to many of the great gardens of the world. Whether this is done on a large or small scale, identical repeated plantings can be used to emphasize or exaggerate perspective along a pathway, entrance or succession of steps. A row of identically planted pots can bring a sense of continuity to a space that seems chaotic and unbalanced, but it can also provide appeal to an empty space that begs for a simple focus.

Repeated plantings can also be used in beds and borders. Placing a succession of large containers that stand above other plantings will create a stunning focal point, which improves the unity and flow of your garden.

of asymmetrical balance would be a tall, narrow plant flanked by a mid-sized oval plant on one side and a shorter, wider plant on the opposite side. A radial planting has a central

Other Design Considerations

Grouping of Containers

Design principles also apply to the grouping and placement of the containers. With careful positioning, a group of varied and different containers can be arranged together for a greater impact, allowing you the opportunity to implement the principles of balance, shape and proportion along with making the most of their varying heights and styles. With the clever placement and layering of containers, you can fill any gaps left by young plants. As the plants mature, the containers can be moved slightly away from one another, allowing space in between for the plants to fill and the sun to reach the leaves.

Adjusting the heights of the pots is another way to create a more luxurious display. Consider raising some of the containers on upturned pots, pot stands or shelves to offer further interest in your grouping.

Containers are traditionally placed in a triangular outline. This includes a tall or large container in the middle with smaller pots tapering down each side, or a tall container on one end with successively smaller containers sloping down

A container herb garden (above). Desert-themed containers with cacti and succulents (below).

to the other. Formal placements often involve an *even* number of containers, such as a pair of square pots marking the front entrance of a house or two rows of containers forming an allée. A row of hanging plants looks best when all the containers are identical; however, the plantings do not need to be the exactly the same. Cottage gardens, large rustic gardens with wild areas and other informal areas can benefit from a scattering of odd containers. Modern, eclectic and contemporary settings are best suited to repeated plantings with repetition done with an *odd* number of containers as the focal point.

Themes

Individual containers and groups of containers can be designed to follow any theme of your choosing—perhaps a Mediterranean theme, using plants that originate from that area, or a tropical theme of plants that you fancy. A fragrance or aromatherapy garden full of herbs and scented flowers is great for accenting seating areas or for using in window boxes. Each container could contain a different scent, which could be easily moved into place to enhance the mood you wish to set, or one large container could have a number or scents within the easy reach of a comfortable chair. Container gardens lend themselves well to novelty themes, such as a salsa garden, where the plants make up most of the ingredients of your recipe, or a theme that integrates the pots into the design, such as different plant hairdos on pots with faces. Container gardening is also well suited to creating cameo gardens, which are small theme gardens in tucked-away places that are somewhat separated from the main garden.

Containers range from fancy pots and urns of all sizes to wooden barrels, planter and window boxes, hanging baskets, washtubs and bathtubs, raised beds, galvanized metal buckets and even a pair of old boots.

Container Selection

Containers range from fancy pots and urns of all sizes to wooden barrels, planter and window boxes, hanging baskets, washtubs and bathtubs, raised beds, galvanized metal buckets and even a pair of old boots. You can experiment with a number of different pots to see what works best. Anything that is sturdy enough to handle the weight and will not fall over can be used as a container.

Bigger is better. A large container is less susceptible to fluctuations in temperature and requires less frequent watering. Larger containers will provide better protection to any bulbs, perennials, trees or shrubs you are going to over-winter. Choose containers that are at least 30 cm (12") in height and in diameter. Smaller pots can dry out very quickly, and they also restrict the root area and reduce the plants' available resources. Deep-rooted plants will need deeper pots.

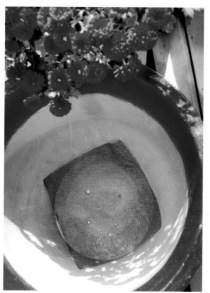

A screen will help prevent soil loss through the drainage holes.

Ensure that any container you use, regardless of the size, has adequate drainage. Containers can be set on bricks or commercially available pot "feet" to help with the drainage. The drainage holes on the bottom of the pot will need to be covered with some material to prevent soil loss. Materials such as fine metal or plastic mesh, newspapers, weed barrier, broken clay flower pot pieces (crocs), coffee filters and cheesecloth are suitable for covering the holes. Many container gardeners will add a 2.5–5 cm (1–2") layer of coarse gravel over the screen to help improve drainage, but this is not totally necessary anymore, as today's plant mixes tend to drain very well. Using gravel, however, will help keep pots stable and will reduce the amount of planting mix needed in the container.

Light-coloured containers are preferable to dark-coloured ones, especially in sunny situations. They will reflect light and will not heat up as much in the sun,

especially in spring when overly warm soil can stimulate early plant growth that could still be damaged by inclement weather. Preventing container heating also helps to prevent roots from cheating or

wheels have a locking mechanism, but it's not always necessary.

Depending on where your container garden is, e.g., on a balcony, you may need to use drip trays or saucers underneath your containers. Saucers are useful in dry parts of the country because they help conserve water use. Saucers are most often made from clay or synthetic materials. Terra-cotta saucers retain moisture and may damage wood or painted surfaces.

Materials

Containers are constructed from a number of different materials including clay, metal, wood, stone and plastic, fibreglass and other synthetics. Be aware that some container materials are more suitable for most parts of our Canadian climate than others.

Some materials are more appropriate for certain containers. Window boxes are usually made out of wood or plastic. Stone or metal are possible, but weight is a critical determining factor. Wooden window boxes can also be custom built

growing to one side of the container. Dark containers are ideal for container designs because they provide a visual anchor like no other tone. Just be cautious as to where and when you use them.

If you plan on moving your containers around, especially large, heavy containers, you may want to have them mounted on wheels. Heavy-duty drip trays, saucers and basic platforms are now available with wheels, allowing you to roll your containers around with relative ease. It's recommended that the

Unglazed terra-cotta pots on the left, and glazed containers on the right.

to blend in with the building architecture. Raised beds are built from wood, brick or stone, and can also be designed to flow with the building architecture and existing landscape. Hanging baskets are most often constructed of wood or wire, with weight again being a determining factor. There are a number of attractive stands available that provide sturdy support for hanging baskets.

Clay

Clay pots come in two basic forms, glazed and unglazed, in a plethora of shapes and sizes. Clay pots can be heavy, even when they are empty. They can be damaged by cold weather and require special care in most parts of Canada, especially in areas that can freeze up rather solidly in the winter as well as in areas that experience numerous freeze/thaw cycles.

Unglazed clay pots are often referred to as terra-cotta, which simply means baked earth, referring to the kiln-firing process used in making the pots.

Clay pots age beautifully over time like no other container material will. Within a few seasons, a combination of salts and organic growth will build on the walls of the pot, resulting in a lovely patina.

Terra-cotta containers are somewhat porous, which allows the plant roots to breathe easily but also allows for the quick evaporation of moisture, so they require frequent monitoring and watering. Terra-cotta holds heat into the night longer than wood, metal or synthetics. Be aware that terra-cotta containers also come in different qualities, and you often get what you pay for. Terra-cotta pots from Italy and other Mediterranean countries are usually very good quality.

Glazed clay containers offer another way to incorporate colour into the overall design scheme of your garden. Glazed containers are not porous, so they will need a few drainage holes on or near the bottom. Glazed pots also benefit from a plastic lining, which helps to prevent cracking if moisture seeps in.

Terra-cotta pots should be soaked before planting. Given its porosity, the clay will draw the moisture out of the soil and away from your new plants.

Wood is great for building window boxes and planters.

Wood

Wooden containers are very adaptable and can be custom-built to fit into their surroundings. Wood offers more insulating value than clay, metal and stone, but it is susceptible to rot, so containers are often lined with plastic or coated with a non-toxic wood preservative. Some woods, such as cedar (*Arborvitae* sp.), are relatively rot resistant. Do not use wood that has been treated with creosote or other toxic substances that can emit compounds that will harm your plants.

Wood is amenable to our climate and can be used across the country. Make sure the containers are of sturdy construction. If you have wooden barrels, make sure the hoops and handles are firmly attached. To ensure the longevity of your wooden containers, protect

them with wood stain, particularly at the joints and seams, or wood oils, both of which enhance the natural grain and prevent it from cracking.

Linseed oil is the best oil to use to protect wood that is prone to drying out.

Stone

Stone includes terrazzo, concrete, reconstructed or refurbished stone and natural stone. Stone containers are available in a vast array of shapes, sizes, styles and colours. They tend to be quite heavy and difficult to move. It is best to plant stone containers after they are set in their relatively permanent location, unless they've been placed atop a strong platform or cart with wheels. Stone is often used to accent gardens, and aggregate planters allow stone to be seen on the container surface. Carved stone pots can be very expensive but will add a level of elegance to any formal container garden. A large rock with a trough makes a wonderful place for tiny alpine plants but may need drainage holes drilled through the stone. Concrete containers, as well as reconstructed and refurbished stone containers, can be cast in many forms. Stone containers are suitable for all areas of Canada.

You can accelerate the aging process on the exterior of your stone containers by simply rubbing a fistful of fresh grass across the surface of the pot. The stain will quickly fade to brown. Brushing a thin layer of yogurt onto a pot's surface will encourage algae and lichen to grow, but a shady and moist location is necessary for the best result.

Stone trough planters (above). A large aggregate container (below).

Metal

Metal containers can be made from tin, copper, bronze, iron, steel or lead, and they range from simple buckets to fancy, ornate planters and urns. Be aware that metal pots absorb heat like dark-coloured containers do. Most metal pots should be lined with plastic or protected from contact with the soil to prolong the longevity of the container, and make sure your metal containers have adequate drainage holes. Plants in plastic containers can be inserted into decorative metal containers rather than using a lining.

Wire is used to make cage-like frames such as hanging baskets, planters and ornate plant stands that can double as planters. These frames are lined with sphagnum moss or some other suitable material before being planted.

To protect the drainage holes from rust, apply a coat of anti-rust paint.

To maintain the bright, reflective surfaces of your metal pots, use a soft cloth and window-cleaning spray. Do not use abrasive pads or cleaners. Be careful not to splash water or potting mix onto polished metal; the splashes may leave white calcium deposits, but they can be removed with a soft cloth.

Synthetic

The most commonly used synthetic materials for containers are plastic and fibreglass. These containers come in a vast range of shapes and sizes, from whimsical plastic duck and teddy bear planters to the newer fibreglass containers that resemble terra-cotta containers. Synthetic containers are not permeable, so they will need drainage holes. They are lightweight and easy to move with minimal concern for breakage, and most of them are good quality and inexpensive. Some lower-quality plastic containers can deteriorate in the sunlight.

Synthetic containers are a good choice for the apartment or condo dweller. They are lightweight and well suited for use on a balcony, and they can be easily moved back and forth seasonally.

Synthetic containers come in all shapes and sizes.

Potting-mix stains, dirty handprints and general muck can be easily removed from most synthetic materials by simply using a soft cloth and soapy water. For tougher stains a scouring pad may be necessary, but test a small, hidden area first in case it will damage the surface.

Container Gardening Rules

Sunlight

Where you choose to place your containers will determine the amount of sunlight they receive. Fortunately, many containers can be easily moved to accommodate the plant's need for more or less sunlight. Often the intensity of the sun can be amplified by the use of reflective materials around the containers.

Four levels of light may be present in your container garden: full sun, partial shade, light shade and full shade. Available light is affected by the position of the sun depending on the time of day and year, as well as by nearby buildings, trees, fences and other structures. Knowing what light is available in your garden will help you determine where to place your containers.

Full-sun locations, such as along south-facing walls, receive direct sun for at least six hours a day. Locations classified as partial shade, such as east- or west-facing walls, receive direct morning or late-afternoon sun and shade for the rest of the day. Light shade locations receive shade for most or all of the day, but some sunlight does filter through to ground level. An example of a light-shade location is the ground under a small-leaved tree such as a birch. Full shade locations, such as under a dense tree canopy, receive no direct sunlight.

Sun-loving plants may become tall and straggly and flower poorly in too much shade. Shade-loving plants may get scorched leaves, or even wilt and die, if they get too much sun. Many plants tolerate a range of light conditions.

It is important to remember that the intensity of full sun can vary. For example, heat can become trapped and magnified between buildings, baking all but the most heat-tolerant plants. Conversely, a shaded, sheltered space that protects your heat-hating plants in the humid, hot summer may become a frost trap in winter, killing tender plants that should otherwise survive.

Exposure

Your garden is exposed to wind, heat, cold and rain, and some plants are better adapted than others to withstand the potential damage of these forces. Buildings, walls, fences, hills, hedges, trees and even tall perennials often reduce exposure.

Wind and heat are the most likely elements to cause damage to your plants, and cold can affect the survival of perennials, trees and shrubs. The sun can be very intense, and heat can rise quickly on a sunny afternoon, so only use plants that tolerate or even thrive in hot weather in the hot spots in your garden. Plants can be dehydrated in windy locations if they aren't able to draw water out of the soil fast enough to replace what is lost through the leaves. Tall, stiff-stemmed plants can be knocked over or broken by strong winds. Some plants that do not require staking in a sheltered location may need to be staked in a more exposed one.

Too much rain can damage some plants, as can overwatering. Established plants (or their flowers) can be

A full sun location (above). A dark container in partial shade (below).

destroyed by heavy rain. Most plants will recover, but some are slow to do so. Grow-covers are used to build temporary greenhouses, usually with a couple of wire hoops placed over the container and a light, white fabric covering is placed over the wires, which allows sun, air and moisture in and keeps bugs, birds and wet weather out. For exposed

Hanging baskets are often very exposed to the environment.

sites, choose plants or varieties that are quick to recover from rain damage. Many of the small-flowered petunia varieties and new petunia cultivars available recover well from the effects of heavy rain.

All hanging baskets are particularly exposed to wind and heat. Water can evaporate from all sides of a moss basket, and in hot or windy locations, moisture can be depleted very quickly. Watch for wilting and water regularly. Wire baskets will hold up better in adverse conditions if you soak the moss or other liner in a commercially available wetting agent, which can be organic, and add some of the wetting agent to the water when first watering.

Use plants that are recommended for exposed locations, or temper the effect of the wind with hedges or trees. A solid wall creates wind turbulence on the downwind side, while a looser structure, such as a hedge, breaks up the force of the wind and protects a larger area.

One drop of a mild liquid dish detergent in one litre of water is a useful and cost-efficient wetting agent. The soap breaks down the surface tension of the water, which allows it to penetrate the material rather than just roll over the outer edge. This is helpful when you're unable to find wetting agents at your garden centre.

Frost Dates and Hardiness Zones

Depending on the types of plants you choose to grow and the types of containers you have, you will need to be aware of frost dates and hardiness zones. Many plants are hardy enough to survive winter outdoors in a large enough container, and many others grow to a mature size in a single season.

When planting annuals, consider their ability to tolerate an unexpected frost. Last-frost and first-frost dates vary greatly from year to year and region to region in Canada. They can also vary considerably within each region. Consult your local garden centre for more specific information.

Annuals are grouped into three categories based on how tolerant they are of cold weather: hardy, half-hardy or tender. Hardy annuals tolerate low temperatures and even frost. They can be placed in your containers early in the year and may continue to flower long into fall or even winter. Many hardy annuals can be seeded directly into containers before the last spring frost date.

Half-hardy annuals can tolerate a light frost but will be killed by a heavy one. These annuals can be planted into your containers around the last-frost date and will generally benefit from being started early from seed indoors,

Nasturtiums and dahlias are tender plants that appreciate protection from frost.

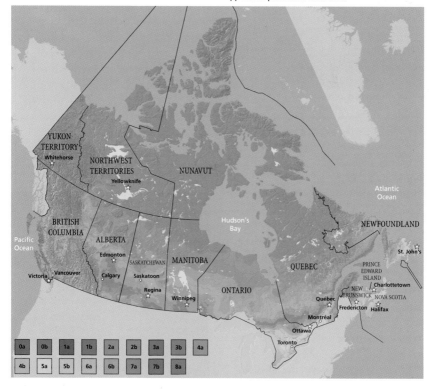

Trees and stairwells can create a microclimate for your containers.

map using recent climate data and incorporating elevation effects.

Canada has a wide range of hardiness zones, and you will need to know the hardiness zone of your part of the country. If you're not sure, ask at your local nursery or a savvy gardener friend.

Don't feel intimidated or limited by the information you'll find on hardiness zones. The divisions are based mostly on the average lowest winter temperatures. Mild or harsh winters, heavy or light snow cover, fall care and the overall health of the plants that you grow all influence their ability to live through winter.

As well, local topography in the garden creates microclimates, small areas that may be more or less favourable for growing different plants. Microclimates may be created, for example, in the shelter of a nearby building or a stand of evergreen trees, in a low, still hollow or the top of a barren, windswept hill or near a large body of water. Microclimates can raise the zone a notch and allow gardeners the possibility of growing a plant that everyone says won't grow in a particular area. Container gardening with plants that are borderline hardy is a challenging and fun part of gardening. Always continue to experiment and explore.

such as those transplants available from garden centres.

Tender annuals have no frost tolerance at all and might suffer if the temperature drops to even just a few degrees above freezing. These plants are often started early indoors and are not planted in the garden until the last-frost date has passed and the ground has had a chance to warm up. These annuals often have the advantage of tolerating hot summer temperatures.

Perennials, bulbs, trees and shrubs have a minimum temperature for survival and will have a hardiness zone designation. These plants will perish if the plants experience a prolonged spell of colder weather. Agriculture Canada scientists created the Canadian hardiness zone map based on minimum winter temperatures and Canadian plant survival data among other variables. Natural Resources Canada's Canadian Forest Service recently updated the hardiness

PROVEN WINNERS

Perennials and shrubs for sale.

Container Principles

Choosing Healthy Plants

Many gardeners consider the trip to the local garden centre to choose their plants an important rite of spring. Others consider starting their own plants from seed one of the most rewarding aspects of gardening. Both methods have benefits, and many gardeners use a combination of the two.

Purchasing plants is usually easier than starting from seed and provides you with plants that are well grown and often already in bloom. Starting seeds can be fun but a little impractical at times. It requires space, facilities and time. Some seeds require specific conditions difficult to achieve in a house, or they have erratic germination rates. Other seeds are easy and inexpensive to start. As well, starting from seed offers you a greater selection because seed catalogues have many more plants available than what is offered at most garden centres.

Purchased plants are grown in a variety of containers. Regardless of the size or age of the plant you're considering for your garden, most plants get established and grow quickly once they are planted in your containers. Most plants are sold in individual pots and in divided cell-packs. Each type has its advantages and disadvantages.

The plant on the right is much healthier than the plant on the left (above). A root-bound rootball (below).

Plants in individual pots are usually well established, having been nurtured along in the nursery, and have plenty of space for root growth. The cost of labour, pots and soil can be expensive if you are purchasing a large number of plants. If you are planting a large container garden, you may also find it difficult to transport large numbers of these plants. Potted plants come in many sizes.

Annuals, biennials and perennials grown in cell-packs are often inexpensive and hold several plants, making them easy to transport. These annuals suffer minimal root damage when transplanted, but because each cell is quite small, plants may become root-bound quickly and should be planted soon after you've purchased them.

Although smaller plants are more economical in the long run, it will take them longer to fill the container. For those of us who reside in a region of Canada with a short season, this may not work, as the containers may not be full and lush until late into the growing season.

Sometimes it's best to purchase plants that haven't yet flowered, but this isn't always a possibility, as many plants are strategically grown to be flowering as early as possible for the garden centres. Plants that haven't yet flowered are younger and less likely to be root-bound. Plants covered with an abundance of flowers or flower buds have already passed through a significant portion of their rooting stage, and while they will add instant colour when planted, they will not perform at their best in the heat of summer, and their longevity can be compromised. Now this is not to say that you shouldn't consider blooming plants for your containers, but if you choose to buy annuals or perennials already in bloom, pinch off the blooms and buds just prior to planting. This encourages new root growth and a bigger show of flowers throughout the season.

Check for roots emerging from the holes at the bottom of the cells, or gently remove the plant from the container to look at the roots. An overabundance of roots means that the plant is too mature for the container, especially if the roots wrapped around the inside of the container resemble a spool of thread. Such plants are slow to establish once they are transplanted into the garden. Healthy roots will appear almost white. Avoid potted plants with very dark, spongy roots that pull away with little effort.

Plants should be compact and have good colour. Healthy leaves look firm and vibrant. Unhealthy leaves may be discoloured, chewed or wilted. Tall, leggy plants have likely been deprived of light. Check carefully for diseases or insects. Do not purchase a diseased plant. If you find insects on the plant, you may not want to purchase it unless you are willing to cope with the insects you are transporting home. To avoid spreading insect pests and diseases, deal

with any problems with the plant before you transplant it into your garden.

Once you get your plants home, water them if they are dry. Plants growing in small containers may require watering more than once a day. Keep them in a lightly shaded location until you plant them. Remove any damaged growth.

Get your plants from a reputable source or, more specifically, a garden centre. Mail-order catalogues, friends, family and neighbours are other sources for plants. A number of garden societies promote the exchange of plants and seeds, and many public gardens sell seeds of rare plants. Gardening clubs are also a great source for rare and unusual plants.

Staff at nurseries and garden centres should be able to answer questions, make recommendations and assist you with whatever you need. It will be helpful to them if you bring an overhead sketch of the area you intend to have

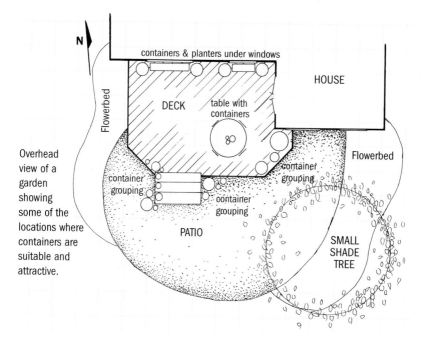

N

containers & planters under windows

HOUSE

Flowerbed

DECK

table with containers

Flowerbed

Overhead view of a garden showing some of the locations where containers are suitable and attractive.

container grouping

container grouping

container grouping

container grouping

PATIO

SMALL SHADE TREE

your container garden and mark potential locations of the containers. Be sure to mark shaded areas, windy areas and the areas that are south-, north-, east- and west-facing so that the professionals can help you choose appropriate plants. You will also find it convenient to take this book to the nursery. You'll have information about the plants and photos of them at your fingertips as you browse.

Preparing Containers for Planting

Container Cleaning

Starting with a clean container is important for minimizing soil-borne plant diseases and for removing deposits from fertilizers and plant root compounds released by the plant into the surrounding soil. Even new containers should be cleaned to remove any dust from transport and handling. Most containers are easily cleaned with mild soap and water with a good rinsing.

Terra-cotta pots require a different cleaning process. Soak the containers overnight or longer in a solution of nine parts water to one part bleach. Soaking the containers for a longer period of time makes the pots easier to clean. Use a plastic bucket appropriate for the size of container you are cleaning. Use a wire or stiff-bristle plastic brush to give the inside of the container a good scrubbing. Deposits can be scraped off with a knife or other appropriate scraping tool. Soak the scrubbed container in clean water for 15 minutes to remove the bleach and then give it a quick spray rinse. If you are cleaning glazed containers, make sure the glaze will not be damaged by the bleach.

Container Drainage

If your container does not have adequate drainage, you run the risk of drowning your plants. Some form of opening in the bottom of containers is essential for good drainage. Extra holes may need to be made in some containers that do not drain as quickly as needed.

Containers that have no drainage, or very minimal drainage, can be used to grow plants that do well in boggy conditions, such as those found along stream banks, ponds and other water features. Decorative containers can also be used just as they would indoors, where a planted pot can easily be dropped into a decorative pot. Ensure that the plants have adequate drainage so water is never allowed to collect or pool between the two pots; otherwise, the rootball will become waterlogged and begin to rot. This arrangement is only recommended for smaller containers.

Choosing a Planting Mix

Many plants need soil that allows excess water to drain away but still retains enough water and nutrients for the plants to use. Commercially available container planting mixes allow good drainage, are lighter in weight than garden soils, have nutrient-holding capacity and do not have soil-borne diseases or weed seeds. Avoid using garden soil because it drains poorly and tends to dry into a solid mass. A small amount

A selection of planting mixes.

of good garden soil can be mixed to add minerals and microorganisms and to improve nutrient holding capacity, but you may also be introducing soil-borne diseases. There are a variety of mixes available depending on what properties your soil needs to have for the plants you want to grow.

Many commercial planting mixes now contain compost in varying percentages. High-quality compost should be an integral part of every container planting mix. Commercial mixes are also available with water-holding polymers already mixed in.

Regular commercial planting mixes are mainly peat moss or coir fibre and can contain tree bark, vermiculite, perlite, dolomite lime, sterilized loam or clay, superphosphate for quick rooting and often some form of slow-release fertilizer. Coir fibre is made from the husks of coconuts. It is more environmentally friendly than peat moss but can be harder to handle. Commercially available organic plant mixes are available in different formulations depending on what the manufacturer chooses to use in the product. They are mainly peat moss or coir fibre and may contain high-quality compost, composted leaf mold, bone meal, blood meal, humus, earthworm castings, bird or bat guano, glacial rock dust, dolomite lime, pulverized oyster shells, alfalfa meal, rock dust, rock phosphate, greensand, kelp meal and beneficial mycorrhizal fungi.

If you plan on having a large number of containers, large bags and bales of commercial planting mix are available. You can also make your own from bulk ingredients to reduce your costs. For the mix we suggest using 40% sphagnum peat moss or coir, 40% high-quality compost, 10% garden loam and 10% washed and screened coarse, angular sand. You can add in high-phosphorous guano or bone meal for a root booster and dolomite lime or oyster shells to raise the pH, or you can mix in a commercially formulated organic fertilizer. Add these fertilizer products as instructed on the product label for the volume of soil your containers will use. A soil test is a useful tool for determining what additions and adjustments your planting mix might need.

Reducing the Weight of Your Containers

Containers can be heavy and steps can be taken to reduce the weight of your containers. Do not use gravel in the bottom of the containers and do not use planting mixes that contain soil or sand. If you will only be planting annuals in larger containers, some of the planting mix in the bottom half can be replaced. You can add in Styrofoam packing peanuts, broken pieces of Styrofoam packing from goods such as electronic products, well-crushed pieces of newspaper or shredded leaves, or you can use flipped over plastic pots set in place before the planting mix is added. Perennials and shrubs, however, may need all the container space filled with soil for roots to grow in.

Planting Your Containers

Generally, you can transplant into containers at the same time you would in a regular garden. There is a proper order to plant into containers. For plants, it is trees first, then shrubs, bulbs, perennials and finally annuals. For size, the largest plants go in first and work down in size to the smallest plants.

Fill your cleaned container with moistened planting mix until it is approximately 75% filled. Place the plants into their respective positions before even removing them from the nursery pots to confirm their orientation in the arrangement. Once you've chosen where they're to go, begin working from the middle of the display outward to the pot's edge. After removing the rootballs from the pots, gently break the outside of the rootballs apart or score the outer roots with a sharp knife to encourage the roots to spread out rather than continuing to coil into a

A selection of plants for a new container (top). Place mesh screen over drainage holes (bottom).

mass. Place the larger, central focal plants into the container first, followed by the smaller ones. Add more potting mix, as necessary, to surround the rootballs of the plants. Add the smallest and

Fill the container with an appropriate amount of planting mix (above). Place still-potted plants in the container to check placement (centre).

Remove plants from their pots and deal with any excess roots (below).

outer-edge plants last and add the last of the potting mix, allowing at least 5 cm (2") from the top edge of the pot for watering. Ensure the planting mix is without gaps or air pockets in between or under any of the plants. This can be done by gently tapping the bottom of the pot on the floor or by slipping your hand into the potting mix to move the soil into gaps and pockets. Watering will also encourage the potting mix to settle without having to firm it down with your hands. Water until the container is thoroughly soaked. Add more planting mix if it settles too much after the first soaking. This is also the time to install trellises, stakes and other supports that are needed.

Don't plant too deeply or too shallowly. Use the depth that the plants are already growing at as a guide for how deeply they should be planted. You don't want to have exposed roots above soil level, but you don't want to bury the crowns, which can lead to rot. If you're adding seeds to the mix, then this should be done at this stage and planted at the depth recommended on the seed package.

How many plants to include in a container is a matter of preference, but overplanted containers look better than having a small number of plants. The spacing between plants in containers can be reduced from what is noted on the plant tag. However, too many plants in one container will be forced to compete with each other for space, water, nutrients and light, so you will still need some soil between each plant to provide room for their roots to spread. Be aware that with more plants in a container you will have to apply more water and fertilizer.

Water plants regularly when they are first planted. Containers can dry out

Tease out some of the roots on the bottom of the root ball (top & centre left).

Make sure each plant has enough room (bottom).

Water the freshly planted container immediately (centre right).

quickly, and newly planted plants need to become established before they can tolerate adverse conditions.

You may find it helpful to make detailed notes and planting diagrams for each container, including when the container was planted and the common and scientific name of each plant for future reference. This is especially helpful when you want to replicate what you planted from one year to the next, based on your successes and failures.

Planting Trees and Specimen Plants

Ensure that the size of the container is of sufficient size to allow for root growth, and include enough planting mix to insulate the roots and crown from extreme climate conditions. Planting mixes for trees benefit from having garden loam as part of the mix. This makes the container more stable and gives the tree roots something a little more solid to root into.

Most plants, especially trees, shrubs and perennials, should be planted in spring to early summer to allow them enough time to become established before facing a Canadian winter. This is, of course, if you want to overwinter the hardy plants in the containers. Some gardeners prefer to keep the hardier plants in the containers for only the growing season with plans to plant them in the ground later on. Others simply want to treat these plants as annuals rather than overwinter them.

Container Garden Maintenance

Your container garden will need regular maintenance just like regular gardens, but on a much-reduced scale. The most important tasks are watering and feeding. Weeding, grooming, relieving soil compaction and repotting are other tasks that require some attention. You will need a minimal selection of quality tools including a hand trowel, a hand cultivator, a watering can with a diffuser, and by-pass hand pruners.

Watering

Watering cans or buckets are good if you have only a small number of containers. Rainbarrels are great places to fill watering cans and buckets. Watering cans come with a diffuser that turns the water flow into a gentle rain shower, which helps lessen soil compaction. A hose with a watering wand is effective for a larger number of containers. You can use commercially available water-holding polymers, which are mixed into the planting mix and act as a moisture reservoir, to reduce your watering time and cost.

Containers will need to be watered more frequently than plants growing in

Organic amendments (left to right): moisture-holding granules, earthworm castings, glacial dust, mycorrhizae, bat guano, compost, bone meal and coir fibre.

Water until it drains freely out the drainage holes.

the ground. The smaller the container, the more often the plants will need watering. Containers, especially hanging baskets and terra-cotta containers, may need to be watered twice daily during hot, sunny and/or windy weather. Water until the entire planting mix is thoroughly soaked and water runs out of the drainage holes. To check if the container needs water, first feel the surface. If it is dry, then poke your finger into the planting mix. If it still feels dry, it is time to water. If the container feels light, it probably needs to be watered.

To save time, money and water, or if you plan to be away from your garden for an extended period, consider installing a drip irrigation system. Drip irrigation systems apply water in a slow, steady trickle, which takes somewhat longer than watering with a can or hose but still thoroughly soaks the containers. Drip irrigation reduces the amount of water lost to evaporation. Systems can be fully automated with timers and moisture sensors. Consult with your local garden centre or irrigation professionals for more information.

You can lower your watering requirements by adding a thin layer of mulch to each container. You can also group containers together to aid in the reduction of evaporation from each container. Placing containers in sheltered locations can also reduce evaporation.

Feeding

Plants in containers have limited access to nutrients. Your plants may need a boost during the growing season, and you will have to apply some form of fertilizer. Plants that are heavy feeders will definitely need additional supplements. Commercially available fertilizer comes in various forms including liquids, water-soluble powders, slow-release granules or pellets and bulk materials such as compost. Follow the package directions carefully because using too much fertilizer can kill your plants by burning their roots. If you use a good-quality planting mix that has compost and an organic or slow-release fertilizer mixed in, you may not need to add extra fertilizer.

Many plants will flower most profusely if they have access to enough nutrients. Some gardeners fertilize hanging baskets and container gardens every time they water, using a very diluted fertilizer so as not to burn the roots. Too much fertilizer stimulates excessive plant growth and can result in lanky stems and weak or overly lush plant growth that is susceptible to pest and disease problems. Some plants, such as nasturtiums, grow better without fertilizer and may produce few or no flowers when fertilized excessively.

Healthy soil allows plants to grow better over the course of summer. Organic fertilizers enhance the micro-organism population in the planting mix, which in turn makes more nutrients available to the plants. Organic fertilizers don't work as quickly as many inorganic fertilizers, but they often don't leach out as quickly. They can be watered into planting mix or used as a foliar spray as often as weekly.

Organic fertilizers can be simple or complex formulations. They may include alfalfa pellets, well-composted animal manure, crab meal, coconut meal, corn gluten, kelp meal, sunflower meal, rock phosphate, humus, leaf mold, bone meal, blood meal, earthworm castings, bird or bat guano, dolomite lime, pulverized oyster shells, glacial rock dust, greensand and beneficial mycorrhizal fungi. Be aware that bonemeal, fish emulsion and other odorous organic fertilizers may attract unwanted garden visitors that can cause major destruction.

Containerized trees and shrubs benefit from the annual removal of some of the planting mix from the top, replaced with fresh, good-quality compost.

Pinching off a spent bloom.

Weeding

Weeding your containers is easiest when the weeds are small. Well-planted containers often exclude enough sunlight to suppress weed growth. Also, don't forget about the weeds that pop up around your containers.

Grooming

Good grooming helps keep your container plants healthy and neat, makes them flower more profusely and helps prevent many pest and disease problems. Grooming may include pinching, trimming, staking, deadheading, training vines and climbing plants and pruning trees and shrubs.

Pinching refers to removing by hand or with scissors any straggly growth and the tips of leggy plants. Plants in cell-packs may develop tall and straggly

Don't be afraid to trim any plant that is exceeding its boundaries (above).

Keep trailing stems from touching the ground.

If annuals appear tired and withered by mid-summer, try trimming them back to encourage a second bloom. Mounding or low-growing annuals, such as petunias, respond well to trimming. Use garden shears and trim back a quarter to half of the plant growth. New growth will sprout along with a second flush of flowers. Give the plants a light fertilizing as well at this time.

Some plants have very tall growth and cannot be pinched or trimmed. Instead, remove the main shoot after it blooms, and side shoots may develop.

Tall plants may require staking. Tie plants loosely to tall, thin stakes with soft ties that won't cut into the plant. Narrow ties are less visible. Stake bushy plants with twiggy branches. Insert the twigs into the planting mix near the plant when it is small, and as the plant grows it will hide the twigs. A careful selection of twiggy branches can add another attractive dimension to your containers.

Vines in containers can be used as trailers or trained to climb up trellises, netting or other structures. These are either inserted into the container, or the container is placed near the structure. Vines with tendrils climb best on structures that are small enough in diameter for the their tendrils to easily wrap around, such as a cage-like trellis or netting. Other climbers will need to be woven through or tied to their structures. Do not be afraid to clip off any rampant or out-of-bounds growth.

Many annuals and perennials benefit from deadheading (removing faded flowers), which often helps prolong their bloom. Deadheading keeps the plants and your containers looking their best

growth in an attempt to get light. Pinch back the long growth when transplanting to encourage bushier growth. Remove any yellow or dying leaves. Pinch back excess growth from more robust plants if they are overwhelming their less vigorous container mates.

Learn proper pruning techniques before trimming trees and shrubs.

and prevents your containers from becoming a seed bank. Decaying flowers can harbour pests and diseases, so it is a good habit to pick off spent flowers when you are checking your containers. Some plants, such as impatiens and wax begonias, are self-cleaning or self-grooming, meaning that they drop their faded blossoms on their own. Leaving the seedheads on some plants, such as ornamental grasses, can provide winter interest.

Trees and shrubs will need to be pruned to keep them healthy and in proportion to the container. Each tree or shrub will have its own pruning requirements, such as the best time to prune and how much of the tree or shrub can be safely removed. It is important to learn where, when and how to make proper pruning cuts. There are books available that describe proper pruning techniques, and classes on pruning are available from horticultural college and university extension programs and public gardens.

Relieving Soil Compaction

Planting mixes in containers can experience soil compaction from the effects of constant watering. A hardened crust on the surface does not allow water and air to penetrate into the planting mix, which can be easily broken up with a good hand cultivator. Replace the top layer of planting mix in spring.

Trees, shrubs and perennials will eventually outgrow their containers.

The top growth (leaves, twigs and branches) of trees and shrubs produces hormones that stimulate root growth, and the roots produce hormones that stimulate top growth.

Repotting Plants

Trees, shrubs and perennials can stay in containers for a number of years with proper care and maintenance. At some point the plants will become rootbound in their containers and will need repotting. Perennials should be divided at this time, and trees and shrubs will need their roots pruned.

Perennials need dividing when flowering is diminished, when the plant loses vigour, when the centre of the plant appears to have died out or when the plant encroaches on the other plants in the container. Replant perennial divisions as soon as possible. Extra divisions can be spread around into other containers, shared with friends or composted. Trees and shrubs that need repotting will also appear less vigorous and have reduced flowering.

The rule of thumb for choosing new containers is to use the next larger size. Perennials will be divided, so they may not need a larger container. Trees and shrubs will require a container only a few centimetres wider and deeper than their current containers, and they will need some root pruning. Using too large a container can cause overwatering problems.

PROVEN WINNERS

Tree and shrub containers can be heavy, and you may need help to tip the container over. Gently remove the plant from the container and shake out some of the old planting mix. You may want to wrap the branches in a blanket to prevent damage to the plant before you tip the container over. Tease out the larger roots that are encircling the container or growing in toward the centre of the root mass and cut them off where they would have just touched the edges of the previous container. When tree roots are pruned or damaged, the plant responds by reducing its top growth. Allow the plants to do this naturally; wait and then prune off the dead branches when they become visible rather than pruning immediately. Replant the tree or shrub into its new home with fresh planting mix, ensuring it is firmly settled with no air pockets.

Pests and Diseases

Your container garden may experience attacks from pests and diseases. This need not be a traumatic event, as there are numerous ways of dealing with any problems that arise. You should not have to worry about soil-borne pests and diseases; they are almost non-existent in container gardens, especially when using soil-less planting mixes.

Annuals are planted each spring, and different species are often grown each year, so it can be difficult for pests and diseases to find their preferred host plants and establish a population. On the other hand, if you grow a lot of one particular annual species, any problems

Green lacewings are beneficial predators.

that do set in over summer may attack all the plants.

Perennials, trees and shrubs are both an asset and a liability when it comes to pests and diseases. Containers often contain a mixture of different plant species. Because many insects and diseases attack only one species of plant, mixed containers make it less likely that pests and diseases will find their preferred hosts among the many other plants to

Aphids.

Adult ladybird beetle.

establish a population. The plants are in the same container for a number of years, and any problems that do develop can become permanent. Yet, if allowed, beneficial insects, birds and other pest-devouring organisms can also develop permanent populations.

IPM (Integrated Pest [or Plant] Management) is a moderate approach for dealing with pests and diseases. The goal of IPM is to reduce pest problems to levels of damage acceptable to you. Attempting to totally eradicate pests is a futile endeavour. Consider whether a pest's damage is localized or covers the entire plant. Will the damage kill the plant, or is it only affecting the outward appearance? Can the pest be controlled without chemicals?

IPM includes learning about your plants and the conditions they need for healthy growth. Some plant problems arise from poor maintenance practices. For example, overwatering saps plants of energy and can cause yellowing of the plant from the bottom up.

It is also useful for you to learn what pests might affect your plants, where and when to look for those pests and how to control them. Keep records of pest damage because your observations can reveal patterns useful in spotting recurring problems and in planning your maintenance regime.

Prevention and Control

The first line of defence for your plants is to prevent pests and diseases from attacking in the first place. The best way to accomplish this is to provide the conditions necessary for healthy plant growth. Healthy plants are able to fend well for themselves and can sustain some damage. Plants that are stressed or weakened are more subject to attack. Begin by choosing pest-resistant plants. Keep your soil healthy by using plenty of good-quality compost. Spray your plant's foliage with high-quality, fungally-dominated compost tea or fish emulsion. This acts as a foliar feed and also prevents against fungal diseases.

Other cultural practices can help prevent pest attacks. Provide enough space for your plants so that they have good air circulation around them and are not stressed from competing for available resources. Remove plants that are decimated by pests and dispose of diseased foliage and branches. Keep your gardening tools clean and tidy up fallen leaves

Powdery mildew.

Ladybird beetle larva.

and dead plant matter in and around your permanently planted containers at the end of every growing season.

Physical controls are generally used to combat insect and mammal problems. An example of such a control is picking insects off plants by hand, which is easy if you catch the problem when it is just beginning. Large, slow insects are particularly easy to pick off. You can squish or rub off colonies of insects with your fingers. Other physical controls include traps, barriers, scarecrows and natural repellants that make a plant taste or smell bad to pests. Garden centres offer a wide array of such devices. Physical control of diseases usually involves removing the infected plant or parts of the plant in order to keep the problem from spreading.

Biological controls make use of populations of natural predators. Birds, spiders and many insects help keep pest populations at a manageable level. Encourage these creatures to take up permanent residence in or near your garden, even though it may be difficult on balcony and rooftop gardens. Bird

baths and feeders encourage birds to visit your container garden and feed on a wide variety of insect pests. Many beneficial insects are already living in or near your garden, and you can encourage them to stay and multiply by planting appropriate food sources. Many beneficial insects eat nectar from flowers.

Chemical controls should be used only as a last resort. Pesticide products can be either organic or synthetic. If you have tried the other suggested methods and still wish to take further action, try to use organic types, available at most garden centres.

Chemical or organic pesticides may also kill the beneficial insects you have been trying to attract. Many people think that because a pesticide is organic, they can use however much they want. An organic spray kills because it contains a lethal toxin. NEVER overuse any pesticide. When using pesticides, follow the manufacturer's instructions carefully and apply in the recommended amounts only to the pests listed on the label. A large amount of pesticide is not any more effective in controlling pests than the recommended amount.

Terra-cotta pots are subject to frost and cold damage.

Protecting Containers and Plants

Frost Damage

Clay containers are subject to frost damage. Any water that has been absorbed by the container will expand as it freezes, causing cracks and chipping. Avoid any containers with narrow openings. When moist soil in the container is subjected to freezing temperatures it will expand, which can crack even the most sturdy clay or stone container. An opening that is equal to or larger than the rest of the container will allow freezing soil to expand upward rather than out.

Insulating Containers

Some plants prefer a cool, moist root environment during the heat of summer and some plants need extra protection

Containers with small openings might not allow freezing soil to expand.

from the effects of winter. Containers can be insulated in similar fashion for both situations. Some materials are better insulators than others. Rot-resistant wood such as cedar makes an attractive container that offers protection from excessive heating and cooling. Other containers may need help in keeping the roots cool. One container placed into another with a minimum of 2.5 cm (1") of space between the containers for insulating material such as moistened vermiculite, sawdust or Styrofoam packing peanuts is effective. The inside of a container may be lined with stiff foam insulation for straight-sided containers or lined with a couple of layers of carpet underlay for curved-sided containers. West Coast gardeners, because of their mild climate, can use a couple of overlapping layers of bubble wrap.

Storing Containers

Containers that will be emptied at the end of the growing season can be cleaned and moved to a suitable storage spot. This will help prolong the life of the containers. Containers that can't be moved and have no plants can be emptied of planting mix and cleaned. Ensure all containers are in good condition, and if needed, repairs can be done during the winter months. Clay containers, especially decorative glazed containers, should be emptied of soil and stored indoors.

Hardy Trees, Shrubs and Perennials

When the outside temperature drops to below 0° C (32° F), the planting mix can freeze solid. Plants continue to use water throughout winter, and even hardy plants can be killed, as frozen planting mix does not allow the plants to take up moisture. Containers that have a large enough volume of planting mix will increase the chances of the plants surviving winter. Water dry containers as soon as the planting mix thaws.

Protecting Tender Plants

Protecting plants from frost is relatively simple. Cover them overnight with sheets, towels, burlap, row covers or even cardboard boxes. Refrain from using plastic because it doesn't retain heat and therefore won't provide your plants with any insulation. You can also move your containers to a frost-free area, such as a garage, garden shed or greenhouse. Tender plants, including tropicals, may have to be moved indoors in winter. Tender evergreen plants can be lifted or dug from their respective containers, repotted and brought into the shelter of a greenhouse or the sunniest, warmest location in your house before the first frosts occur in fall. Most tender plants can be treated as houseplants, whether they return outdoors the following season or not. If you're without space to overwinter large, tender plants indoors, cuttings can be taken in late summer and grown as smaller plants for the following spring.

Overwintering Tender Rhizomes, Bulbs, Corms and Tubers

Perennials that grow from tender rhizomes, bulbs, corms or tubers can be dug up in fall after the top growth dies back, stored over winter and replanted in spring. If there is a chance that the container may freeze, dig up the tubers, bulbs, rhizomes, or corms before that can happen. Shake the loose dirt from the roots and let them

Make sure the container is big enough to protect the plant's roots (left). This might not be the best storage for terra-cotta containers (right).

dry in a cool, dark place. Once dry, the rest of the soil should brush away. You can dust the roots with an antifungal powder, such as garden sulphur (found at garden centres), before storing them in moist peat moss or coarse sawdust. Keep them in a cool, dark, dry place that doesn't freeze. Check on them once a month, and lightly spray the storage medium with water if they appear very dry. If they start to sprout, pot them and keep them in moist soil in a bright window. They should be potted by late winter or by early spring so that they will be ready for the outdoors. Some gardeners will leave the tubers, etc., in the containers and store the whole containers inside over winter.

All in all, container gardening is foolproof. There's little commitment with container gardening because you can change styles, plants, design or composition from one season to the next, or more importantly, from one year to the next. Container gardening offers valuable lessons as to what plants prefer as far as cultural conditions, their growth habits and appearance. It is cost and time efficient, and it can cater to every gardener's need. You may even find that once you embark on gardening in containers, you'll find it difficult to stop. So don't be afraid to try something new, experiment and have fun. With this in mind, you cannot fail.

PROVEN WINNERS

PROVEN WINNERS

About this Guide

This book showcases 116 plants suitable for container gardening in Canada. The plants are organized alphabetically by their most familiar common names. Additional common names and scientific or botanical names appear after the primary reference and in the **Features** section. This system enables those who are familiar with only the common name of a plant to find that plant easily in the book. The scientific or botanical name is always listed (in italics), and readers are strongly encouraged to learn these botanical names. Common names are sometimes shared by several different plants, and they can change from region to region. Only the true botanical name defines the specific plant everywhere on the planet.

The illustrated **Plants at a Glance** section at the beginning of the book allows you to quickly familiarize yourself with the different plants, and it will help you to find a plant if you're unsure of its name.

Clearly indicated within each entry are the plant's height and spread ranges, outstanding features and hardiness zone(s). At the back of the book, you will find a **Quick Reference Chart** that summarizes different features and requirements of the plants; you will find this chart handy when planning what is best for your container gardening designs.

Each entry gives clear instructions for planting and growing the plants in a container garden and recommends many of our favourite selections. Note: if height and spread ranges or hardiness zones are not given for each and every recommended plant, assume these values are the same as the ranges at the beginning of the entry. If unsure, check with your local garden centre experts when making your selections.

Finally, pest and disease issues that may come about are addressed in the **Pests and Diseases** section of the introduction, which provides information on how to recognize, diagnose and solve these problems.

PROVEN WINNERS (OPPOSITE PAGE)

Plant Directory

Aeonium

Aeonium

A. arboreum 'Zwartkop'

Some stems form a solitary rosette, while others produce a colony or cluster of rosettes.

Also called: saucer plant **Features:** glossy or semi-glossy, green, bronze, brown, purple or near-black foliage; sometimes small, bright yellow, star-shaped flowers **Height:** 30–90 cm (12–36") **Spread:** 30–45 cm (12–18") **Hardiness:** tender perennial overwintered indoors

Aeonium forms attractive rosettes of glossy, succulent foliage. Clusters of star-shaped flowers are produced from the rosettes, after which that rosette often dies.

Growing

Aeonium grows well in **full sun** or **light shade**. The potting mix should be **moist** and **well drained**. This plant prefers to be watered regularly but is fairly drought tolerant if you occasionally skip watering. Fertilize every two weeks during the growing season with quarter-strength fertilizer. This tender, slow-growing plant can be moved indoors in winter.

Tips

Aeonium is an eye-catching addition to mixed containers. It is ideal for themed containers, where it often forms the focal point with its dark foliage. Mix it with grasses and even cacti for a southwestern look or with other Mediterranean plants for a mini-vacation in a planter. It is a good choice for container gardeners who don't always remember to water as often as they should.

Recommended

A. arboreum is sparsely branched with glossy, leathery leaves arranged in rosettes at the ends of the branches. The foliage is green with purple, bronze or brown margins and mid-ribs. '**Zwartkop**' ('Schwarzkopf'), a Proven Winners Selection, has very dark purple, nearly black, foliage.

African Lily
Agapanthus

A. campanulatus hybrid

ven when not in bloom, African lily contributes clumps of bright green foliage to mixed containers, providing a lush background for companions with lots of flowers but sparse foliage or for taller plants with leggy lower limbs.

Agapanthus is derived from the Greek words agape, *meaning "love," and* anthos, *meaning "flower."*

Growing

African lily grows well in **full sun, partial shade** or **light, dappled shade.** Provide protection from the hottest afternoon sun. The potting mix should be **moist** and **well drained.** Roots may rot in poorly drained containers. Fertilize weekly with half-strength fertilizer during the growing season.

Also called: lily-of-the-Nile **Features:** clump-forming perennial; bright green, strap-like leaves; purple, blue or white, mid- to late-summer flowers **Height:** 30–90 cm (12–36") **Spread:** 30–45 cm (12–18") **Hardiness:** zones 7–8

A. *campanulatus* hybrid (above & below)

Move containers to a sheltered location during frosty weather where plants are hardy. They can be lifted in fall and stored for re-planting in spring or stored in their containers in a cold but frost-free location in areas where they are not hardy.

Tips
African lilies make excellent filler plants. The strap-like leaves are bright green, and the rounded or pendulous clusters of flowers atop long, straight stems make excellent companions to flowering shrubs and large, shrub-like perennials.

Recommended
A. 'Blue Triumphator' forms a dense clump of foliage and bears loose clusters of bright blue flowers.

A. 'Bressingham White' forms a dense clump of foliage and bears loose clusters of white flowers.

A. campanulatus forms a dense clump of grey-green foliage and produces loose clusters of flowers in shades of blue, purple or sometimes white. 'Albovittatus' has white-margined leaves.

A. 'Lilliput' is a dwarf hybrid that grows 30–45 cm (12–18") tall with an equal spread. It bears rounded clusters of deep blue flowers.

African lilies have flowerheads known as umbels, which are large and rounded and made up of many tubular flowers.

Angel's Trumpet

Brugmansia, Datura

*A*ll angel's trumpets add an exotic accent to the garden with their elegant, trumpet-shaped flowers.

Growing

Angel's trumpet grows best in **full sun**. The potting mix should be **moist** and **well drained**. Fertilize every two weeks with quarter- to half-strength fertilizer during the growing season.

Tips

Angel's trumpet flowers tend to open and be most fragrant at night. Place them in containers where you will enjoy them in the evening—near a patio, on a balcony or on a deck. They make excellent companions for other annuals.

Recommended

B. **x** *candida* (*B. aurea* x *B. versicolor*) is a large, woody plant that can grow up to 3 m (10') tall in a container and can be pruned to keep it smaller. It bears fragrant, white flowers that often open only on summer evenings. Cultivars are available, including '**Grand Marnier,**' with apricot-coloured flowers; '**Golden Queen,**' with yellow, double flowers; and '**Purple Queen,**' with white and purple, double flowers.

D. metel is an annual plant that easily self-seeds. It grows 90 cm–1.2 m (3–4') tall and wide and produces white flowers in summer. '**Cornucopia**' has purple and white, double flowers.

D. metel with petunias and impatiens

Angel's trumpets are frost-tender, but B. x candida *can be overwintered in a bright, cool room indoors.*

Also called: datura, trumpet flower, jimsonweed **Features:** bushy growth; white, yellow or purple, trumpet-shaped flowers **Height:** 60 cm–3 m (2–10') **Spread:** 60 cm–1.2 m (2–4') **Hardiness:** tender annual; woody shrub grown as an annual

Arborvitae

Thuja

T. plicata SPRING GROVE, a Proven Winners Color Choice Selection

Arborvitae can only be grown in containers for three to five years, after which it will need to be planted in the ground, or it is likely to die.

Also called: cedar **Features:** evergreen shrub or small tree **Height:** 45 cm–3 m (18"–10') **Spread:** 45 cm–1.2 m (18"–4') **Hardiness:** zones 3–8

This beautiful evergreen, with soft foliage that won't poke you in close quarters, has dozens of dwarf cultivars that can last for several years in a big enough container.

Growing

Arborvitae grows well in **full sun, partial shade** or **light shade** in a sheltered location. The potting mix should be moist and **well drained**. Keep plants well watered. Fertilize with a weak fertilizer no more than monthly in spring and early summer. Overwinter outdoors in a location out of strong winds and bright sun. Both can dry the foliage out and kill the plant.

Tips

Arborvitae is popular for use as a screening plant on decks and patios. It can be grown alone or combined with flowering perennials and annuals. The larger the container the better, as this woody plant consumes a lot of water.

Recommended

T. occidentalis (eastern white cedar) is a large, pyramidal tree with scale-like, evergreen needles. Many cultivars suitable for containers are available. **'Danica'** is a dwarf globe form growing to about 45 cm (18") tall and wide with bright emerald green foliage. **'Emerald'** is narrow and upright and is considered one of the hardiest cultivars, more so if it doesn't dry out in winter. It grows about 3 m (10') tall and 90 cm (36") wide before it needs transplanting to a garden. **'Hetz Midget'** is a rounded dwarf cultivar. It grows 60 cm–1.2 m (2–4') tall and wide and can be pruned to maintain a smaller size. More dwarf cultivars are available.

T. plicata (western red cedar) is a fantastic, huge tree native to western North America, but a few dwarf cultivars are small enough for containers. This species and its cultivars are only hardy to zone 5. **'Cuprea'** is a low, mound-forming cultivar with bright yellow-tipped, bronzy green foliage. It grows about 90 cm (36") tall and wide. **'Whipcord'** has long, pendulous, rope-like foliage that gives the plant a mop-like appearance. It grows about 90 cm (36") tall and spreads about 75 cm (30").

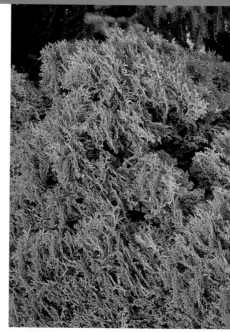

T. occidentalis cultivar (above)
T. occidentalis 'Danica' (below)

Argyranthemum
Argyranthemum

The daisy-like flowers seem to suit almost any setting.

Growing
Argyranthemums prefer **full sun** but tolerate partial shade with decreased flowering. The potting mix should be **well drained**. Fertilize monthly with half-strength fertilizer during the growing season. Pinch the plants back early on to encourage bushy growth.

Tips
Argyranthemums can be used in mixed containers, as an accent to specimen plants or to add a colourful splash. They are lovely when massed in large container groupings or in window boxes on a sunny ledge.

Recommended
A. fructescens is a compact, rounded plant. It bears single, yellow-centred, white-petalled, daisy-like flowers. 'Butterfly,' a Proven Winners Selection, produces canary yellow flowers. 'Gypsy Rose' bears single, yellow-centred flowers with dark pink petals. 'Molimba Helio Double Pink' bears light pink, double flowers that have a tufted appearance. 'Vanilla Butterfly' bears single, yellow-centred, daisy-like flowers with creamy white petals that are pale yellow at the base.

A. fructescens 'Butterfly' with million bells, sedum and others

Also called: cobbity daisy **Features:** bushy habit; white, pink or yellow, summer flowers; divided to finely divided foliage
Height: 40–90 cm (16–36")
Spread: 60–90 cm (24–36")
Hardiness: subshrub grown as an annual

Cuttings can be taken in late summer and grown indoors over winter to be used the following summer.

Asparagus Fern
Asparagus

A. densiflorus 'Sprengeri' with begonias

Asparagus fern is actually not a fern, but a member of the lily family. It is closely related to edible asparagus.

Growing

Asparagus fern grows best in **light shade** or **partial shade** with protection from the afternoon sun. Avoid deep shade and direct sunlight. The potting mix should be kept evenly **moist**, but allowed to dry out a little between waterings. Fertilize weekly with quarter- to half-strength fertilizer during the growing season. It must be overwintered indoors or thrown away at the end of the season.

Tips

Vigorous growth makes asparagus fern a good filler plant for mixed containers, while its unique appearance and habit add an interesting visual element to any combination.

Recommended

A. densiflorus is an arching, tender perennial with light green, feathery, leaf-like stems. Two cultivars are commonly available. **'Myersii'** (foxtail fern) produces dense, 30–45 cm (12–18") long, foxtail-like stems. **'Sprengeri'** (emerald fern) has bright green, arching to drooping stems and a loose, open habit. It spreads 90 cm– 1.5 m (3–5') and is often grown where it will have room to hang.

Features: fern-like habit; bright green, needle-like or narrow, leaf-like stems; inconspicuous flowers; inedible, red berries **Height:** 30–90 cm (12–36") **Spread:** 30 cm– 1.5 m (1–5') **Hardiness:** tender perennial grown as an annual

Athyrium
Athyrium

A. niponicum var. *pictum* with iris, heucherella and others

The demand for athyrium will certainly encourage enthusiastic breeders to create more varieties of this popular plant.

Features: deciduous, perennial fern; decorative foliage **Height:** 30 cm–1.2 m (1–4')
Spread: 30 cm–1.2 m (1–4')
Hardiness: zones 4–8

Athyrium is one of the few ferns really suitable for container culture: delicate, decorative and well behaved.

Growing
This fern grows well in **full shade, partial shade** or **light shade**. The potting mix should be **acidic** and **moist**. Fertilize every two weeks with quarter-strength fertilizer. It will need some protection in winter. Cover it if it will be

left outdoors, or move it to a sheltered location.

Tips

Create a woodland understorey in a pot. Combine hosta, coral bells, annabelle hydrangea and athyrium in a large planter for a shaded location. Athyrium makes an attractive addition to almost any mixed planter combination and will perform admirably as long as it doesn't get too much sun.

Recommended

A. felix-femina (lady fern) forms a dense clump of lacy fronds. The appearance can be quite variable, as the leaflets on the fronds and the fronds themselves are prone to dividing, giving the plants a more lacy appearance or sometimes even a dense, ball-like appearance. It varies in size from dwarfs that grow 30 cm (12") tall and wide to plants that can grow 60 cm–1.2 m (2–4') in height and spread. Interesting cultivars include **'Dre's Dagger,'** with narrow leaflets arranged in four rows around each frond, and **'Encourage,'** whose leaflets are divided at the tips, giving a frilly or fan-like appearance to the outer edges of each frond. Hard to find in Canada, but interesting nonetheless, is **'Acrocladon,'** whose fronds subdivide so often that the fern appears to be a small, dense ball of foliage.

A. niponicum var. *pictum* (Japanese painted fern) is a low, creeping fern with reddish to burgundy stems and a silvery metallic sheen to the bronzy fronds. Several cultivars have been developed with varied frond colours. **'Burgundy Lace'** has pinkish purple fronds with a metallic sheen. **'Silver Falls'** has silvery metallic fronds with striking, reddish purple stems and veins.

A. niponicum 'Silver Falls' (above)
A. felix-femina (below)

Bacopa
Sutera

S. cordata 'Snowstorm Giant Snowflake' with osteospermum and fan flower

Bacopa grows under and around the stems of taller plants, forming a dense carpet dotted with tiny flowers, and eventually drifts over pot edges in a cascade of stars.

Growing

Bacopa grows best in **partial shade** with protection from the hot afternoon sun. The potting mix should be **moist** and **well drained**. Don't allow this plant to completely dry out; the leaves will die quickly if they become dry. Cutting back dead growth may encourage new shoots to form.

Features: white, lavender, purple, blue or pink flowers; decorative foliage; trailing habit **Height:** 8–15 cm (3–6") **Spread:** 30–60 cm (12–24") **Hardiness:** tender perennial grown as an annual

Tips

Bacopa is a popular plant for hanging baskets, mixed containers and window boxes. It forms an attractive, spreading mound.

Recommended

S. cordata forms a dense, compact mound of heart-shaped leaves with scalloped edges and bears tiny, white, star-shaped flowers along its neat, trailing stems. '**Cabana Trailing Blue**' bears blue or purple flowers. '**Lavender Showers**' bears pale lavender flowers. '**Olympic Gold**' has gold variegated foliage with white flowers. '**Snowstorm Giant Snowflake**,' a Proven Winners Selection, is a vigorous plant with large, white flowers. '**Snowstorm Pink**' has light pink flowers.

Basil
Ocimum

The sweet, fragrant leaves of fresh basil add a delicious, licorice-like flavour to salads and tomato-based dishes.

Growing

Basil grows best in a warm, sheltered location in **full sun**. The potting mix should be **moist** and **well drained**. Fertilize weekly with half-strength fertilizer. Pinch tips and remove flower spikes regularly to encourage bushy growth.

Tips

Combine basil in a mixed container with other moisture-loving plants, or consider combining several different types of basil.

Recommended

O. basilicum is one of the most popular of the culinary herbs. There are dozens of varieties, including ones with large or tiny, green or purple, smooth or ruffled leaves, as well as varied flavours including anise, cinnamon and lemon. **'Green Globe'** forms a rounded mound of tiny leaves. **'Mammoth'** has huge leaves, up to 25 cm (10") long and about half as wide. **'Purple Ruffles'** has dark purple leaves with frilly margins. **'Siam Queen'** is a cultivar of Thai basil with dark green foliage and dark purple flowers and stems.

O. basilicum 'Genovese' and *O. basilicum* 'Cinnamon'

Although basil will grow best in a warm spot outdoors, it can also be grown successfully in a bright window indoors to provide you with fresh leaves all year.

Features: bushy habit; fragrant, decorative leaves; pink, purple or white flowers
Height: 30–60 cm (12–24")
Spread: 30–45 cm (12–18")
Hardiness: tender annual

Bay Laurel
Laurus

L. nobilis

This shrub is an undemanding plant that is happily transferred from a sunny window indoors to a lightly shaded spot outdoors when the weather allows.

Growing
Bay laurel grows well in **light shade, partial shade** or **full sun** in a sheltered location. The potting mix should be **moist** and **well drained**. Fertilize monthly with half-strength fertilizer. Plants will need to be overwintered indoors in all but the very warmest parts of Canada.

Tips
Bay laurel is an attractive, small shrub, useful as a structural point in a mixed container and equally attractive when grown as a specimen. It can be pinched back to maintain a compact form or trained as a standard. Combine it with other herbs for a themed container or group of themed containers.

Recommended
L. nobilis is an aromatic, evergreen tree that can grow up to 12 m (40') tall where it is hardy. In a container it stays much smaller and can be pruned to maintain a suitable size. **'Aurea'** has golden yellow foliage.

Bay leaves are familiar to most of us as the large, flat leaves we pick out of our stews or soups before serving.

Also called: sweet bay **Features:** tender, evergreen shrub; neat habit; undemanding
Height: 30–90 cm (12–36")
Spread: 20–60 cm (8–24")
Hardiness: zone 8

Begonia
Begonia

B. x *tuberhybrida* cultivar with rubber plant, licorice plant, coleus, phormium and lamium

With beautiful flowers, a compact or trailing habit and decorative foliage, there is sure to be a begonia to fulfill your shade-gardening needs.

Growing

Begonias prefer **light to partial shade**, though wax begonias are quite sun tolerant. The potting mix should be **neutral to acidic, humus rich** and **well drained**. Mix some compost into a peat-based potting mix. Fertilize every two weeks with quarter- to half-strength fertilizer.

The tubers of tuberous begonias can be uprooted when the foliage dies back and

Begonias have attractive, colourful foliage. Combine rex begonias with silver-leaved lamium or grey-leaved licorice plant for contrasting colour.

Features: bushy habit; decorative foliage; red, pink, orange, yellow, apricot or white, sometimes bicoloured (picotee) flowers **Height:** 15–60 cm (6–24") **Spread:** 15–60 cm (6–24") **Hardiness:** tender perennial grown as an annual

stored in slightly moistened peat moss over winter. The tuber will sprout new shoots in late winter and can be potted for another season. Rex begonias can be moved indoors and treated as houseplants in winter.

Tips

All begonias are useful for containers and planters on shaded patios, balconies, decks and porches. The trailing, tuberous varieties can be used in hanging baskets where the flowers can cascade over the edges.

Recommended

B. **Rex Cultorum hybrids** (rex begonias) are dense, mound-forming plants with dramatically patterned, high-contrast variegated foliage in shades of green, red, pink, white, bronze or purple. **'Escargot'** has spiraling, silver-striped, bronzy green leaves. **'Fire Flush'** has red-tinged, green and bronze variegated leaves. **'Fireworks'** has silvery white and purple-banded foliage. **'Wineuma'** has bright green leaves with scarlet undersides.

B. x *tuberhybrida* (tuberous begonias) form bushy mounds with green, bronze or purple foliage. The flowers can be held upright or in pendulous clusters. There are many hybrids of tuberous begonias available. **Non-stop Series** begonias are compact, bushy plants with red, yellow, apricot, orange, pink or white, double flowers. Two pendulous selections are **'Chanson,'** with single or semi-double flowers, and **'Illumination,'** with fully double flowers. Both have flowers in a wide range of colours.

B. hybrid (above), *B.* x *tuberhybrida* cultivar with phormium and others (below)

Bidens

Bidens

A. ferulifolia 'Peter's Gold Carpet'

With fern-like foliage and pretty, golden flowers, this plant has a delicate appearance that belies its tough nature.

Growing

Bidens prefers **full sun** but will tolerate partial shade, bearing fewer flowers. The potting mix should be **moist** and **well drained**. Fertilize every two weeks with quarter- to half-strength fertilizer.

If plants become lank and unruly in summer, shear them back lightly to encourage new growth and fall flowers.

Tips

Bidens is an absolute must for containers, window boxes and hanging baskets. Its fine foliage and attractive flowers make it useful for filling spaces between other plants.

Recommended

B. ferulifolia is a short-lived perennial that is used as an annual. Tufts of fernlike foliage are tipped with daisy-like, bright yellow flowers. **'Golden Goddess'** bears slightly larger flowers and narrower leaves. **'Peter's Gold Carpet,'** a Proven Winners Selection, is a bushy, wide-spreading selection with deep golden yellow flowers. **'Solaire Compact Yellow'** is a low-growing plant with a mounding rather than trailing habit.

Features: bushy habit; feathery foliage; bright yellow flowers **Height:** 30–60 cm (12–24") **Spread:** 30–90 cm (12–36") or more **Hardiness:** tender perennial grown as an annual

Black-Eyed Susan

Rudbeckia

R. hirta

As a cut flower, black-eyed Susan is long lasting in arrangements.

Features: short-lived perennial; summer through fall flowers in shades of yellow, orange, brown, red or gold, with brown or green centres **Height:** 45 cm–3 m (18"–10')
Spread: 30–90 cm (12–36")
Hardiness: zones 2–8; treated as an annual

Bright and cheerful, black-eyed Susan provides a summer-long display of colourful flowers.

Growing
Black-eyed Susan grows well **in full sun** or **partial shade**. The potting mix should be **well drained**. Water regularly, though plants are fairly drought tolerant. Fertilize monthly with half-strength fertilizer.

Pinch plants in June to encourage shorter, bushier growth. Deadhead to keep the plants neat and to encourage more flower production.

Tips

Black-eyed Susan is a floriferous addition to mixed containers. It is good to use in wildflower- or native-themed containers. As well, it isn't unruly and won't become lank, floppy or messy, as some plants often do if grown in containers.

Recommended

R. hirta (gloriosa daisy) forms a bushy mound of bristly foliage and bears bright yellow, daisy-like flowers with brown centres from summer through to the first hard frost in fall. **'Becky'** is a dwarf cultivar that grows up to 30 cm (12") tall and has large flowers in solid and multi-coloured shades of yellow, orange, red or brown. **'Cherokee Sunset'** was a 2002 All-America Selections winner. It bears semi-double and double flowers in all colours. **'Irish Eyes'** bears bright yellow flowers with green centres. This cultivar grows 60–75 cm (24–30") tall and is best in large containers where it will not look out of proportion. **Toto Series** is a group of bushy dwarf cultivars that grow 30–40 cm (12–16") tall and bear single flowers with central brown cones with golden orange, lemon yellow or rich mahogany petals.

There are many more hybrids and species of black-eyed Susan. Most grow 90 cm–1.8 m (3–6') tall, making them less suitable for containers, though certainly worth a try if you are looking for a big plant to make a bold statement.

R. hirta with dahlia, sedum, fan flower and sedge (above), *R. hirta* 'Irish Eyes' (below)

Black-Eyed Susan Vine
Thunbergia

T. alata (far left)

Black-eyed Susan vine is a useful vine whose simple flowers dot the plant, giving it a cheerful, welcoming appearance.

Growing
Black-eyed Susan vine grows well in **full sun**, **partial shade** or **light shade**. The potting mix should be **moist** and **well drained** and have some organic matter such as earthworm castings or compost mixed in. Fertilize every two weeks with quarter-strength fertilizer during the growing season. It can be brought into the house over winter then returned to the garden the following spring—it is a perennial treated as an annual.

Tips
Black-eyed Susan vine can be trained to twine around railings and up trellises and small obelisks. It is attractive trailing down from mixed containers and hanging baskets.

Recommended
T. alata is a vigorous, twining climber. It bears yellow flowers, often with dark centres, in summer and fall. **'African Sunset'** was released in 2002 with flower colours that range from deep brick red to warm pastel colours to cream. **'Alba'** bears white flowers with dark purple-brown centres. **Suzie hybrids** bear large flowers in yellow, orange or white.

Features: twining, evergreen vine; attractive foliage; yellow, orange, white or sometimes red, summer to fall flowers **Height:** 90 cm–1.5 m (3–5') **Spread:** 30 cm–1.5 m (1–5') **Hardiness:** tender perennial grown as an annual

Blood Grass

Imperata

Blood grass appears to glow red when backlit by the sun during the day or by a spotlight at night.

Growing

Blood grass grows best in **full sun** or **partial shade.** The potting mix should be kept **moist** but not wet. Mix in compost or earthworm castings, as this grass likes organic matter in its soil. Fertilize every two weeks with quarter-strength fertilizer during the growing season. Pull out any growth that doesn't turn red, as green growth is more vigorous and will tend to dominate. Cover containers or move them to a sheltered location in winter.

Tips

Blood grass mixes well in a grass-themed container and makes a good upright companion for bushy and trailing perennials and annuals. Its small size and non-invasive habit are welcome in mixed containers where more vigorous grasses can easily overwhelm other plants.

Recommended

I. cylindrica **var.** *rubra* (I. cylindrica 'Red Baron') forms slow-spreading clumps of slender leaves. The grass blades emerge bright green tipped with red that spreads down the leaf as it matures, turning deep wine red by fall, then to copper in winter.

Blood grass is great to brighten up containers, adding a textural element offered by few other plants.

I. cylindrica var. *rubra* with ipomoea and spirea

Also called: Japanese blood grass
Features: perennial grass; colourful foliage; slender, upright habit **Height:** 30–45 cm (12–18") **Spread:** 30 cm (12")
Hardiness: zones 4–8

Blue Oat Grass
Helictotrichon

H. sempervirens

Looking like a giant pincushion, blue oat grass has a strong architectural presence.

Growing
Blue oat grass thrives in **full sun**. The potting mix should be **well drained**. This grass thrives in poor soil and should only be fertilized once at the beginning of summer with half-strength fertilizer. Cover containers or move them to a sheltered location in winter.

Tips
The bushy, rounded form lends itself perfectly to being grown as a specimen in a large, urn-shaped container. It can also be combined with perennials and annuals as the centrepiece in a mixed container.

Recommended
H. sempervirens forms a large, dome-shaped clump of narrow, silvery blue leaf blades. Wiry, tan stems emerge from the centre of the clump, bearing feathery, tan seedheads. **'Saphirsprudel'** ('Sapphire,' 'Sapphire Fountain') is sometimes described as being larger and more intensely blue than the species, while some growers claim they can see no difference between the species and the cultivar.

Blue oat grass is a tough, hardy grass, one of the most likely to survive winter in a large container.

Features: perennial grass; cushion-like habit; brilliant blue foliage; decorative spikes of tan seedheads
Height: 60 cm–1.2 m (2–4')
Spread: 60–75 cm (24–30")
Hardiness: zones 3–8

Bougainvillea

Bougainvillea

Each tiny bougainvillea flower is surrounded by three wavy, papery bracts. When it's in flower, the blooms can completely cover the plant.

Growing

Bougainvillea grows best in **full sun** but tolerates partial shade or light shade. The potting mix should be **moist** and **well drained**. Mix in compost or earthworm castings. Fertilize every two weeks during the growing season with quarter- to half-strength fertilizer. This tender plant should be overwintered indoors.

Tips

Often purchased as a houseplant, it really thrives when it is moved outdoors in summer. Alone, as a specimen or mixed with other plants, bougainvillea is lovely and adaptable. It can be trained as a trailing spreader, bushy shrub, standard or climbing vine.

Recommended

B. glabra is a tender, evergreen vine with semi-glossy leaves. The bracts may be white or magenta and are produced in mid- and late summer and sometimes again in winter. Where it is hardy it can grow up to 8 m (26') tall. In containers it isn't quite as vigorous and can be kept at a size you can accommodate. There are many hybrids; one that is often available, **'Raspberry Ice,'** has green leaves with irregular, creamy margins. The bracts are bright pink.

Placing an obelisk in the centre of the container to support bougainvillea will benefit this vine as it matures, allowing the other plants surrounding it to be seen and enjoyed rather than obscured by the thorny, twining stems.

B. glabra

Features: evergreen, attractive, sometimes variegated foliage; pink, white, yellow, apricot, red or purple flower bracts
Height: 20 cm–1.2 m (8"–4')
Spread: 30–90 cm (12–36")
Hardiness: tender vine grown as an annual or overwintered indoors

Bugleweed
Ajuga

A. reptans cultivar with a fern

Bugleweed's shade tolerance makes it particularly welcome in urban settings in places with limited sun exposure, such as on balconies and between buildings.

Growing
Bugleweed develops the best leaf colour when grown in **partial shade** or **light shade** but tolerates full shade. Excessive sun may scorch the leaves. Any **well-drained** potting mix is suitable for these plants. Overwinter outdoors in a sheltered location.

Tips
Bugleweed will spread to fill in the spaces between plants in your mixed containers, and some selections will even trail over the edge of the container. The bold, colourful foliage can be used to create striking contrasts. Try planting it at the foot of a shrub rose like Knock Out or with a soft-leaved perennial like lady's mantle.

Recommended
A. genevensis is an upright species that bears bright blue, white or pink flowers.

A. pyramidalis 'Metallica Crispa' is slow-growing, with crinkly, bronze foliage and violet blue flowers.

A. reptans is a low, quick-spreading plant with many colourful cultivars, such as 'Burgundy Glow,' 'Caitlin's Giant' and 'Multicolour.'

A. x tenorii is a hybrid with small leaves, a somewhat trailing habit and deep blue flowers. Available are the cultivars 'Chocolate Chip' and 'Vanilla Chip.'

Features: evergreen perennial; purple, pink, bronze, green or white, often variegated foliage; late-spring to early-summer flowers in purple, blue, pink or white **Height:** 8–30 cm (3–12") **Spread:** 15–90 cm (6–36") **Hardiness:** zones 3–8

Calla Lily
Zantedeschia

Z. elliottiana hybrid with petunias, canna lily, dracaena and Swan River daisy

Calla lilies are exotic and elegant and lend a tropical touch to your container garden.

Growing

Calla lilies grow best in **full sun** in a sheltered location. The potting mix should be **moist** and **well drained** until the leaves have begun to unfurl. Once plants are actively growing, the soil can be kept quite wet. Fertilize every two weeks with quarter- to half-strength

Don't feel you must store all the rhizomes you lift in fall; these plants grow vigorously, and you may need only a few pieces for the following summer. The rest can be given to friends and family or thrown away.

Features: rhizomatous; clump-forming; glossy, green foliage; summer flowers
Height: 40–90 cm (16–36") **Spread:** 20–60 cm (8–24") **Hardiness:** tender perennial grown as an annual

Z. elliottiana hybrid (above), *Z. elliottiana* hybrid with pansies (below)

fertilizer. Deadhead the faded flowers and stems.

Slowly reduce the water toward the end of summer to encourage dormancy and the foliage to die back. After a light frost, remove the foliage and stems from the rhizome, being careful not to damage the roots. Wash the rhizome gently under tepid water, removing soil and debris. Dust the rhizome with a fungicide and leave it to dry for a week at room temperature in a well-ventilated room. Once cured, store the rhizome in a paper bag in a cool, dark location at 5°–10° C (41°–50° F) until it's time to plant it again in spring.

Tips

Calla lilies are stunning additions to large, colourful, mixed or specimen containers. For a theme garden, combine them with other water-loving plants like monkey flower, elephant ears, rush and sweet flag to create a potted bog garden.

Recommended

Z. aethiopica forms a clump of glossy, green, arrow-shaped leaves. Ornamental, white spathes surround the creamy yellow flower spikes. Cultivars and hybrids are available.

Z. elliottiana (yellow calla, golden calla) forms a clump of white-spotted, dark green, heart-shaped leaves. Yellow spathes surround bright yellow flower spikes. This species is the parent plant of many popular hybrids.

Z. rehmannii (pink arum, pink calla) forms a clump of narrow, dark green leaves. White, pink or purple spathes surround yellow flower spikes. This species is also the parent of many hybrids.

Canna Lily
Canna

*C*anna lilies are stunning, dramatic plants that give an exotic flair to any garden.

Growing

Canna lilies grow best in **full sun**. The potting mix should be **moist** and **well drained**. Fertilize every two weeks with quarter- to half-strength fertilizer during the growing season. Deadhead regularly to prolong blooming. Once all of the buds have opened and the flowers are finished, remove the stalk down to the next side shoot.

Lay the rhizomes flat and just barely cover them with soil when planting. Transplant canna lilies earlier than June to ensure they will flower before the end of the season.

Tips

Canna lilies can be included in large planters. They can be grown in containers of mixed canna lily varieties or used as focal points with bushy and trailing annuals.

Recommended

A wide range of canna lilies is available, including cultivars and hybrids with green, bronze, purple or yellow-and-green-striped foliage. Flowers may be white, red, orange, pink, yellow or sometimes bicoloured. **Pfitzer Series** has dwarf selections that grow about 90 cm (36") tall.

C. hybrid with lobelia

The silvery foliage of dusty miller and licorice plant creates an excellent backdrop for the colourful foliage and flowers of canna lily.

Features: rhizomatous; green, blue-green, bronze, purple, yellow or sometimes variegated foliage; red, white, orange, pink, yellow or sometimes bicoloured flowers **Height:** 90 cm–2.1 m (3–7') **Spread:** 45–90 cm (18–36") **Hardiness:** zones 7–8; tender perennial grown as an annual

Catch-Fly

Silene

S. pendula 'Peach Blossom'

Catch-fly helps keep pest populations down by attracting beneficial insects and even by catching small insects on its sticky stems and leaves.

Also called: silene **Features:** bushy, spreading or upright habit; loose or dense clusters of deep to light pink or white flowers **Height:** 15–60 cm (6–24") **Spread:** 15–45 cm (6–18") **Hardiness:** annual

The flowers of this plant are attractive to hummingbirds, butterflies and other pollinating insects.

Growing

Catch-fly grows well in **full sun** or **light shade**. The potting mix should be **moist** and **well drained**. Fertilize every two weeks during the growing season with quarter- to half-strength fertilizer. No worries about overwintering—this plant is an annual.

Tips

Catch-fly makes a good filler plant in mixed containers. This annual may turn up in your containers year after year, as it tends to self-seed.

Recommended

S. armeria (sweet William catch-fly) forms a basal rosette of grey-green leaves from which many sticky stems emerge. It bears clusters of vivid pink flowers. '**Electra**' bears more flower clusters than the species.

S. coeli-rosa (rose-of-heaven) is an upright plant with slender, grey-green foliage. Flowers are bright pink with paler, often white centres. '**Blue Angel**' bears blue flowers. '**Rose Angel**' bears bright pink flowers.

S. pendula (nodding catch-fly) is a low-growing, bushy, mounding or spreading plant. It bears loose clusters of nodding, single or double, light pink flowers. '**Peach Blossom**' has flowers that open a deep pink and gradually fade to white as they mature, with flowers in different stages of colouration showing at once. '**Snowball**' bears double, white flowers.

Cilantro · Coriander

Coriandrum

C. sativum

The delicate, cloud-like clusters of flowers attract pollinating insects such as butterflies and bees as well as abundant predatory insects that will help keep pest insects at a minimum in your garden.

Growing

Cilantro prefers **full sun** but tolerates partial shade. The potting mix should be **light** and **well drained**. Fertilize monthly with half-strength fertilizer. This plant dislikes humid conditions and does best during a dry summer.

Tips

Cilantro has pungent leaves and is best planted where people will not have to brush past it. It is, however, a delight to behold when in flower and is an excellent plant for adding volume to your mixed planters. The airy clouds of white flowers create a lovely backdrop for bright red, pink or purple flowers.

Recommended

C. sativum forms a clump of lacy basal foliage above which large, loose clusters of tiny, white flowers are produced. The seeds ripen in late summer and fall.

This plant is a popular culinary herb. The leaves, called cilantro, are used in salads, salsas and soups, and the seeds, called coriander, are used in pies, chutneys and marmalades. The flavour of each is quite distinct.

Features: form; foliage; flowers; seeds
Height: 40–60 cm (16–24")
Spread: 20–40 cm (8–16")
Hardiness: tender annual

Clematis

Clematis

C. integrifolia

Combine two clematis selections together to provide a mix of tone and texture.

Features: twining vine or bushy perennial; attractive, leafy habit; flowers in shades of blue, purple, pink, white, yellow or red or sometimes bicoloured **Height:** 30 cm–1.5 m (1–5') **Spread:** 30 cm–1.2 m (1–4') **Hardiness:** zones 3–8

Climbing vines can be truly stunning growing up an obelisk or other trellis from a container, and though gardeners have reported mixed results treating clematis this way, the possibility of success makes it worth a try.

Growing

Clematis plants prefer **full sun** but tolerate full shade. Try to keep the container in the shade, as these plants do best when their roots stay cool. The potting mix should be **moist** and **well drained** and have some organic matter like compost mixed in. Fertilize every two weeks during the growing season with quarter- to half-strength fertilizer.

These plants are hardy in many Canadian gardens, but because the roots are quite sensitive, they may survive the winter in a container only if it can be moved to a location where the temperature will stay fairly even. Freezing and thawing will be more likely to kill your clematis vines than extreme cold. Try moving the whole container to an unheated garage or shed.

Tips

Clematis plants make a lovely addition to a mixed container where you can grow them up an obelisk or trellis, or let them spill over the edge. The abundant flowers make these plants worth including in your containers even if they survive only a few years.

Recommended

C. alpina (alpine clematis) is a twining vine that blooms in spring and early summer, bearing bell-shaped, blue flowers with white centres.

C. integrifolia (solitary clematis) is a bushy perennial rather than a climbing vine, though it has flexible, trailing growth that can be trained to grow up a low container trellis. It will spill over the edge of a container and bears flared, bell-shaped, purple flowers in summer.

C. x jackmanii (jackman clematis) is a common, twining vine clematis that bears large, purple flowers in summer. There are many other clematis hybrids with flowers in a wide range of colours available.

C. integrifolia (above), *C. x jackmanii* (below)

Cleome

Cleome

C. *hassleriana* with nicotiana, geranium and impatiens

"Hummingbird flower" might be a more appropriate name for this plant. It blooms through fall, providing nectar for the tiny birds after many other flowers have finished blooming.

Create a bold, exotic display in your garden with these lovely and unusual flowers.

Growing

Cleome prefers **full sun** but tolerates partial shade. The potting mix should be **moist** and **well drained**. These plants are drought tolerant but look and perform best if watered regularly. Fertilize monthly during the growing season with quarter-strength fertilizer. Pinch out the centre of a cleome plant when transplanting, and it will branch out to produce up to a dozen blooms. Deadhead to prolong the blooming period.

Tips

Cleome is an interesting plant to use as the central or focal plant in a mixed container.

Recommended

C. hassleriana is a tall, upright plant with strong, supple, thorny stems. The foliage and flowers of this plant have a strong, but pleasant, scent. Flowers are borne in loose, rounded clusters at the ends of leafy stems. Many cultivars are available.

C. serrulata (Rocky Mountain bee plant) is native to western North America. It is rarely available commercially. The thornless dwarf cultivar **'Solo'** is available to be grown from seed. It grows 30–45 cm (12–18") tall and bears pink and white blooms.

Also called: spider flower **Features:** bushy, upright habit; scented, divided foliage; pink, rose, violet or white flower clusters **Height:** 30 cm–1.5 m (1–5') **Spread:** 45–90 cm (18–36") **Hardiness:** annual

Clover

Trifolium

Because of its small stature, clover can be lost to the eye when mixed with other plants in beds but seems to stand out when planted in containers, both as a specimen or when mixed with other annuals.

Growing

Clover is best grown in **full sun to partial shade**. The potting mix should be **moist, well drained** and **neutral**. Fertilize once during the growing season, about a month after you plant it out, with half-strength fertilizer. Move it to a sheltered location in winter, or throw it away after the first frost and plant new clover the following summer.

Tips

This lovely little plant will add interest to mixed containers. It is especially striking when grouped with other plants with dramatically coloured foliage or bright, contrasting flowers.

Recommended

T. repens is a low, spreading perennial that is often grown as an annual. It is rarely grown in favour of the many attractive cultivars. The small, rounded flower clusters can be pink, red, yellow or white. **'Dark Dancer'** ('Atropurpureum') has a dwarf habit and deep, dark burgundy leaves with lime green margins. **'Salsa Dancer'** produces bright green foliage with burgundy and white markings in the centre of each leaf and white flowers.

Because of its invasive nature, clover is ideally suited to container culture so that it won't be able to stray.

T. repens 'Dark Dancer' with coleus and others

Features: spreading perennial; decorative, often variegated foliage; small, globe-shaped, white, pink, red or yellow flowers
Height: 8–30 cm (3–12")
Spread: 30–45 cm (12–18") or more
Hardiness: zones 4–8; grown as an annual

Coleus

Solenostemon (Coleus)

S. scutellarioides cultivar with coral bells and others

Coleus can be trained to grow into a standard (tree) form. Pinch off the lower leaves and side branches as they grow to create a long, bare stem with leaves on only the upper half. Once the plant reaches the desired height, pinch from the top to create a bushy, rounded crown.

Features: bushy habit; colourful, often variegated foliage in shades of green, yellow, pink, red, burgundy or purple **Height:** 15–90 cm (6–36") **Spread:** 15–60 cm (6–24") **Hardiness:** tender perennial grown as an annual

Coleus has always been available in a great range of colours, and it is only more desirable as new varieties emerge onto the market in colours such as plum, burgundy, chartreuse, gold, lime, copper, wine and almost black.

Growing
Coleus prefers to grow in **light shade** or **partial shade** but tolerates full shade if not too dense and full sun if the plants are watered regularly. The potting mix should be **humus rich, moist** and **well drained**. Mix in some compost or earthworm castings.

These plants are perennials that are grown as annuals, but they also make attractive houseplants. Cuttings taken from favourites in late summer can be grown indoors in a bright room by a sunny window.

Tips

The bold, colourful foliage creates a dramatic display when several different selections are grouped together in a single container or group of containers. Coleus also makes an excellent accent plant in a mixed container with other annuals or perennials.

When flower buds develop, it is best to pinch them off because the plants tend to stretch out and become less attractive after they flower.

Recommended

S. scutellarioides (*Coleus blumei* var. *verschaffeltii*) cultivars and hybrids form bushy mounds of foliage. The leaf edges range from slightly toothed to very ruffled. The leaves are usually multicoloured with shades ranging from pale greenish yellow to deep purple-black. Plants grow 15–90 cm (6–36") tall, depending on the cultivar, and the spread is usually equal to the height. Some interesting cultivars include 'Black Prince,' with deep purple, almost black foliage; 'Fishnet Stockings,' with purple-veined, bright green foliage; 'Merlin's Magic,' with deeply divided, slightly ruffled, purple, pink, burgundy or yellow and green variegated foliage; and SEDONA, a Proven Winners Selection, with pink-veined, orange foliage.

S. *scutellarioides* SEDONA (above)
S. *scutellarioides* cultivar with begonia and fig (below)

Coral Bells

Heuchera

H. DOLCE KEY LIME PIE with sedge and osteospermum (above), *H.* hybrid with ipomoea, begonia and sweet flag (below)

Also called: heuchera, alum root **Features:** mound-forming or spreading perennial; scalloped or heart-shaped, colourful foliage; small, red, pink, purple, white or yellow, summer flowers **Height:** 30 cm–1.2 m (1–4') **Spread:** 30–45 cm (12–18") **Hardiness:** zones 3–8

From soft yellow-greens and oranges to midnight purples and silvery, dappled maroons, coral bells offer a great variety of foliage options.

Growing

Coral bells grow best in **light shade** or **partial shade**. Foliage colours can bleach out in full sun. The potting mix should be **neutral to alkaline, moist** and **well drained**. Mix in some compost or earthworm castings. Fertilize once a month during the growing season with quarter- to half-strength fertilizer. Cover them or move them to a sheltered location in winter.

Tips

Coral bells make attractive additions to mixed containers where the colourful foliage contrasts particularly well with grasses, ferns and yellow-flowered plants like lady's mantle, iris and dahlia. Combine different selections of coral bells for an interesting display.

Recommended

There are many hybrids and cultivars of coral bells available. The following are just a few of the possibilities. **'Caramel'** has apricot-coloured foliage and pink flowers. **'Chocolate Ruffles'** has ruffled, glossy, brown foliage with purple undersides that give the leaves a bronzed appearance. **'Coral Cloud'** forms a clump of glossy, crinkled leaves and bears pinkish red flowers. **'Firefly'** develops a clump of dark green leaves with attractive, fragrant, bright pinkish red flowers. **'Lime Rickey'** and DOLCE KEY LIME PIE, a Proven Winners Selection, form low masses of chartreuse leaves. **'Marmalade'** has foliage that emerges red and matures to orange-yellow. **'Montrose Ruby'** has bronzy purple foliage with bright red undersides. **'Northern Fire'** has red flowers and leaves mottled with silver. **'Obsidian'** has lustrous, dark purple, nearly black, foliage. **'Pewter Veil'** has silvery purple leaves with dark grey veins. Its flowers are white flushed with pink. **'Velvet Night'** has dark purple leaves with a metallic sheen and creamy white flowers.

Coral bells are delicate-looking woodland plants and can be combined with other woodland plants like ferns to create a themed container.

H. AMBER WAVES, from Proven Winners, alone and with osteospermum, in front of sedge (above), *H.* hybrid with pansies, vinca and dracaena(below)

Cranesbill

Geranium

G. JOLLY BEE, a Proven Winners Selection

The decorative foliage of many cranesbills is reason enough to grow them.

Also called: perennial geranium **Features:** clump- or mound-forming perennial; white, red, pink, purple or blue, summer flowers; dense, often deeply divided foliage
Height: 15–90 cm (6–36") **Spread:** 30–90 cm (12–36") **Hardiness:** zones 2–8

Cranesbills are available in a huge range of heights and colours, at least some of which are sure to suit your container garden needs.

Growing

Cranesbills prefer to grow in **partial shade** or **light shade** but tolerate full sun. The potting mix should be **well drained**. Fertilize every two weeks with quarter-strength fertilizer during the growing season. Move containers to a sheltered location protected from temperature fluctuations in winter.

Tips

These long-flowering plants are great in mixed containers. The simple flowers aren't exceptionally showy, but their constant presence is appreciated as other flowers come and go.

Recommended

G. **'Johnson's Blue'** forms a spreading mat of foliage. Bright blue flowers are borne over a long period in summer.

G. x *oxonianum* is a vigorous, mound-forming plant with attractive, evergreen foliage. It bears pink flowers from spring to fall. **'A. T. Johnson'** bears silvery pink flowers. **'Wargrave Pink'** is a vigorous cultivar that bears salmon pink flowers. (Zones 3–8)

G. pratense (meadow cranesbill) forms an upright clump and bears clusters of white, blue or light purple flowers for a short period in early summer. It self-seeds freely. **'Mrs. Kendall Clarke'** bears rose pink flowers with blue-grey veining. **'Plenum Violaceum'** bears purple, double flowers for a longer period than the species. (Zones 3–8)

G. sanguineum (bloody cranesbill, bloodred cranesbill) forms a dense, mounding clump and bears bright magenta flowers mostly in early summer and sporadically until fall. **'Album'** has white flowers and a more open habit than other cultivars. **'Alpenglow'** has bright, rosy red flowers and dense foliage. **'Elsbeth'** has light pink flowers with dark pink veins. The foliage turns bright red in fall. **Var.** *striatum* is heat and drought tolerant. It has pale pink blooms with blood red veins. (Zones 3–8)

G. 'Johnson's Blue' (above)
G. pratense 'Plenum Violaceum' (below)

Crocosmia

Crocosmia

C. 'Lucifer'

The intense colours of crocosmia are a beacon in the garden and create a brilliant display in a container.

Growing

Crocosmias prefer **full sun** in a sheltered location. The potting mix should be **humus rich, moist** and **well drained**. Fertilize plants monthly with half-strength fertilizer. Move plants to a sheltered location in winter where they are hardy. Where they are not hardy, they will need to be moved to a location where temperatures will stay consistently around freezing. These plants will be short-lived in containers.

Tips

These attractive, unusual plants create a striking display when planted by themselves in large containers or in mixed containers with other perennials.

Recommended

C. x crocosmiflora is a spreading plant with long, strap-like leaves. It grows 45–90 cm (18–36") tall, and the clump spreads about 30 cm (12"). One-sided spikes of red, orange or yellow flowers are borne in mid- and late summer. **'Citronella'** ('Golden Fleece') bears bright yellow flowers.

C. **'Lucifer'** is the hardiest of the bunch and bears bright scarlet flowers. It grows 90 cm–1.2 m (3–4') tall, with a spread of about 45 cm (18").

Features: cormus, semi-tender perennial; red, orange or yellow flowers in mid- to late summer; bright green, strap-like leaves
Height: 45 cm–1.2 m (18"–4')
Spread: 30–45 cm (12–18")
Hardiness: zones 5–9

If you've had no luck overwintering crocosmia, the corms can be dug up in fall and stored in slightly damp peat moss in a cool, dark place during winter.

Cuphea
Cuphea

These wonderful plants will attract hummingbirds and butterflies to your garden.

Growing
Cupheas grow well in **full sun** or **partial shade**. The potting mix should be **moist** and **well drained**. Short periods of drought are tolerated. Fertilize monthly during the growing season with half-strength fertilizer.

These plants are tender and can be treated like annuals or brought indoors at the end of summer and treated like houseplants.

Tips
Cupheas are excellent plants for containers of all descriptions. The container can be brought into the house in winter and kept in a sunny window.

Recommended
C. **hybrids** offer a differing selection from the cultivars in subtle ways, including flower colour and habit. A few to watch for are the FLAMENCO SERIES, from Proven Winners, which is made up of FLAMENCO TANGO, with bright purple-pink flowers, and FLAMENCO RUMBA, with fiery red flowers and dark purple centres.

C. **hyssopifolia** (Mexican heather, false heather, elfin herb) is a bushy, branching plant that forms a flat-topped mound. The flowers have green calyces and light purple, pink or sometimes white petals. The plants bloom from summer to frost. **'Allyson Purple'** ('Allyson') is a dwarf plant that bears lavender flowers. **'Desert Snow'** has white flowers.

C. **ignea** (*C. platycentra*; cigar flower, firecracker plant) is a spreading, freely branching plant. Thin, tubular, bright

C. FLAMENCO RUMBA

red flowers are produced from late spring to frost. It can also be used as a houseplant.

The genus name, Cuphea, *arises from the Greek word* kyphos, *meaning "curved." The name refers to the curved seed capsules.*

Features: tropical shrub; red, pink, purple, violet, green or white flowers **Height:** 15–60 cm (6–24") **Spread:** 25–90 cm (10–36") **Hardiness:** tender shrub grown as an annual

Dahlia

Dahlia

D. 'Chic'

Dahlia cultivars span a vast array of colours, sizes and flower forms, but breeders have yet to develop true blue, scented and frost-hardy varieties.

Features: tuberous; bushy habit; attractive foliage; summer flowers in shades of red, yellow, orange, pink, purple or white, or sometimes bicoloured **Height:** 20 cm–1.5 m (8"–5') **Spread:** 20–60 cm (8–24")
Hardiness: tender perennial grown as an annual

The variation in size, shape and colour of dahlia flowers is astonishing. With an estimated 58,000 selections having been developed, you are sure to find at least one or two that you just have to have for your containers.

Growing

Dahlias prefer **full sun**. The potting mix should be **humus rich, moist** and **well drained**. Fertilize every two weeks with quarter-strength fertilizer. Deadhead to keep plants neat and to encourage more blooms.

Dahlias are tender, tuberous perennials that are treated as annuals. The tubers can be lifted in fall and stored over winter in slightly moist peat moss. Pot them and keep them in a bright room when they start sprouting in mid- to late winter.

Tips

Dahlias make attractive, colourful additions to mixed containers. Their sturdy, bushy growth gives them a shrubby appearance that can be used to visually anchor a mixed container that includes softer-looking or trailing plants. The stunning dahlia flowers draw the eye and create a strong focal point, so use them in places you want people to see or notice.

Recommended

D. hybrids are bushy, tuberous perennials with glossy leaves in shades of green, bronze or purple. They are generally described by their flower shape, such as collarette, decorative or peony-flowered. The flowers range in size from 5–30 cm (2–12") and are available in shades of purple, pink, white, yellow, orange, red or bicoloured. Here are a few interesting selections. **'Amazon Pink and Rose'** is a miniature plant with yellow-centred, pink, semi-double flowers. The petals are light pink with deep pink bases. **'Bishop of Llandaff'** has dark red, semi-double flowers and bronze foliage. **'Dalstar Yellow'** is a miniature plant with pale yellow, semi-double flowers. **'Dalina Mini Bahamas'** is a dwarf plant with glossy, green foliage and fuchsia pink, double flowers. **'David Howard'** has multi-tonal orange, double flowers that contrast strikingly with its dark purple foliage. **'Figaro'** can be started from seed and has double and semi-double flowers in a wide range of colours.

D. hybrids with lobelia and dracaena (above)
D. hybrid with zinnia, nasturtium and thyme (below)

Daylily
Hemerocallis

H. 'Stella de Oro'

More than 12,000 daylily selections have been developed, with sometimes hundreds more added yearly.

Features: clump-forming perennial; spring and summer flowers in every colour except blue and pure white; grass-like foliage **Height:** 30 cm–1.2 m (1–4') **Spread:** 30 cm–1.2 m (1–4') **Hardiness:** zones 2–9

The daylily's adaptability and durability, combined with its variety in colour, blooming period, size and texture, explain this perennial's popularity.

Growing
Daylilies grow in any light from **full sun to full shade**. The deeper the shade, the fewer flowers will be produced. The potting mix should be **moist** and **well drained**, but these plants will tolerate both wet and dry conditions. Fertilize

monthly with half-strength fertilizer. Deadhead to encourage more flowering. Move containers to a sheltered location in winter.

Tips

Plant daylilies alone, or group them in containers. Although the small selections seem best suited to container culture, the larger plants make a bold statement and will grow equally well in containers.

Recommended

Daylilies come in an almost infinite number of forms, sizes and colours in a range of species, cultivars and hybrids. They all form clumps of strap-like foliage and produce a cluster of buds on a stem that is held above the foliage. The buds open one at a time, and each lasts for a single day. There are many species and hybrids available. The following are just a sampling of the possibilities.

H. citrina (citron daylily) blooms at night and has dark green foliage. It bears fragrant, trumpet-shaped, narrow-petalled, lemon yellow flowers.

H. 'Eenie Allegro' is a dwarf hybrid with pink-edged, apricot-coloured flowers.

H. 'Pardon Me' is a dwarf hybrid with bright red, ruffled, fragrant flowers.

H. 'Stella de Oro' is one of the best-known hybrids. It is a dwarf plant with golden yellow flowers. It blooms on and off for most of summer.

H. 'Vivacious' has silvery pink, ruffled flowers.

H. 'Dewey Roquemore' (above)
H. fulva 'Flore Pleno' (below)

Dogwood
Cornus

C. sericea 'Isanti'

Moving dogwoods to an unheated garage or shed will protect them from wind and temperature fluctuations in winter in the colder parts of Canada.

Features: deciduous large shrub or small tree; attractive, late-spring to early-summer flowers; fall foliage; stem colour; fruit
Height: 90 cm–3 m (3–10') in containers
Spread: 60 cm–2.4 m (2–8') in containers
Hardiness: zones 2–9

Flowers, stem colour, leaf variegation, fall colour, growth habit, adaptability and hardiness are all positive attributes to be found in dogwoods.

Growing
Dogwoods grow well in **full sun, light shade** or **partial shade**, with a slight preference for light shade. The potting mix should be **humus rich, neutral to slightly acidic** and **well drained**. Mix in compost or earthworm castings and

fertilize monthly during the growing season with quarter-strength fertilizer. Move them to a sheltered location in winter.

Tips

If you have very large containers or planters, you might be wondering if there are any shrubs or small trees you can grow. Dogwoods are a good choice, though they may need a bit more pruning and training than they would in a garden. The larger dogwoods will probably outgrow a container and need to be moved to a garden in about three to five years, unless you root prune them every two or so years.

Recommended

C. alba (red-twig dogwood, Tartarian dogwood) and *C. sericea* (*C. stolonifera*; red-osier dogwood) species and cultivars are grown for their bright red stems that provide winter interest. Cultivars are available with stems in varied shades of red, orange or yellow. Fall foliage colour can also be attractive. (Zones 2–8)

C. alternifolia (pagoda dogwood) can be grown as a large, multi-stemmed shrub or a small, single-stemmed tree. The branches have an attractive, layered appearance. Clusters of small, white flowers appear in early summer. The cultivar **'Argentia'** has silver and green variegated leaves. (Zones 3–8)

C. kousa (Kousa dogwood) is grown for its decorative flowers, fruit, fall colour and interesting bark. The white-bracted flowers are followed by bright red fruit. The foliage turns red and purple in fall. **'Satomi'** has soft pink flowers. (Zones 5–8)

C. alba 'Bud's Yellow' (above), *C. alba* 'Bailhalo' (below)

Dusty Miller
Senecio

S. *cineraria* 'Silver Dust'

Dusty miller makes an artful addition to container gardens. The soft, silvery grey, deeply lobed foliage creates a good backdrop to show off the brightly coloured flowers or foliage of other plants.

Growing
Dusty miller prefers **full sun** but tolerates light shade. The potting mix should be **well drained**. Fertilize no more than once a month with quarter-strength fertilizer. Pinch off the flowers before they

bloom; the flowers aren't showy and steal energy that would otherwise go to the foliage.

Tips
The soft, silvery, lacy leaves of dusty miller are its main feature, and it is used primarily as a contrast or backdrop plant.

Recommended
S. cineraria forms a mound of fuzzy, silvery grey, lobed or finely divided foliage. Many cultivars have been developed. **'Cirrus'** has lobed, silvery green or white foliage. **'Silver Dust'** has deeply lobed, silvery white foliage. **'Silver Lace'** has delicate, silvery white foliage that glows in the moonlight.

Features: bushy habit; variably lobed foliage in shades of silvery grey
Height: 30–60 cm (12–24")
Spread: equal to height or slightly narrower
Hardiness: tender annual

Dwarf Morning Glory
Convolvulus

*I*f you love morning glory but don't want a climber, try this little cutie in containers and window boxes.

Growing

Dwarf morning glory prefers **full sun**. The potting mix must be **well drained**. Fertilize no more than once, about a month after planting, with quarter-strength fertilizer. This plant will produce lots of foliage but few flowers in soil that is too fertile.

Tips

Dwarf morning glory is a compact, mounding plant that can be grown in containers and hanging baskets. It makes a nice plant to grow alone in a small container and also mixes well with other annuals. The mounding to slightly trailing form looks good when combined with grasses.

Recommended

C. tricolor is a compact, mound-forming plant that bears trumpet-shaped flowers that last only a single day, opening in the morning and twisting shut that evening. **Ensign Series** has low-growing, spreading plants that grow about 15 cm (6") tall. **'Royal Ensign'** has deep blue flowers with white and yellow throats. **'Star of Yalta'** bears deep purple flowers that pale to violet in the throat.

C. tricolor

Although this plant is related to the noxious weed C. arvensis *(bindweed), dwarf morning glory is in no way invasive or problematic.*

Features: mound-forming habit; blue, purple or pink, summer flowers sometimes variegated with yellow and white throats **Height:** 15–40 cm (6–16") **Spread:** 25–30 cm (10–12") **Hardiness:** annual

Elder

Sambucus

S. *nigra* BLACK BEAUTY with osteospermum, coral bells and spurge (above), S. *nigra* BLACK LACE (below)

Features: large, bushy, deciduous shrub; early-summer flowers; edible fruit; colourful, decorative foliage **Height:** 60 cm–3 m (2–10') in containers **Spread:** 60 cm–3 m (2–10') in containers **Hardiness:** zones 3–8

Elder is a versatile shrub that can be trained to function as a small tree in a container garden.

Growing

Elders grow well in **full sun** or **partial shade**. Yellow-leaved cultivars and varieties develop the best colour in light shade or partial shade, and black-, burgundy- or purple-leaved cultivars develop the best colour in full sun. The potting mix should be **moist** and **well drained**. Fertilize monthly with quarter-strength fertilizer during summer. Stop fertilizing before fall to give the plant time to harden off for winter. Move containers to a sheltered location for winter or cover them to protect them from wind and temperature fluctuations.

Prune plants back in spring to keep them at a suitable size. You may have to root prune them every few years or move them to a garden when they become too large for the container.

Tips

Elders make a strong architectural statement and are best suited to large containers. Train them as small, single- or multi-stemmed trees. Plant annuals with contrasting flower colours around the base of an elder for an eye-catching combination.

Recommended

S. canadensis (American elder), *S. nigra* (black elder) and *S. racemosa* (European red elder) are rounded shrubs with white or pink flowers followed by red or dark purple berries. Cultivars are available with green, yellow, bronze or purple foliage and deeply divided or feathery foliage, including *S. canadensis* '**Lanciniata,**' with lacy, green foliage that gives this shrub a fern-like or feathery appearance; *S. nigra* BLACK BEAUTY, with dark purple, almost black, foliage that darkens as summer progresses; *S. nigra* BLACK LACE, a Proven Winners Color Choice Selection, produces finely cut black foliage with pink flowers; *S. nigra* '**Madonna,**' with dark green foliage with wide, irregular, yellow margins; and *S. racemosa* '**Sutherland Gold,**' with deeply divided, yellow-green foliage.

Elderberries will attract birds to your garden.

S. *nigra* 'Madonna' (above)
S. *racemosa* 'Goldilocks' (centre)

S. *nigra* BLACK BEAUTY (below)

Elephant Ears
Colocasia

This striking plant will add a tropical look to your patio, deck or balcony.

Growing
Elephant ears grow well in **light shade** or **full shade**. The potting mix should be **humus rich, slightly acidic** and **moist to wet**. Fertilize every two weeks during the growing season with quarter-strength fertilizer. Move elephant ears indoors in winter, or store the tuberous roots in a cool, dry location until spring.

Tips
Planted alone in a moist container or combined with other moisture-lovers, this plant makes a striking addition to any container garden.

Recommended
C. ecsulenta is a tuberous, warm-climate plant that produces a clump of large, heart-shaped leaves. Cultivars with red- or purple-veined to dark purple or bronze foliage are available. **'Black Magic'** has dark purple leaves. **'Fontanesii'** has green leaves with red to purple stems, veins and margins.

C. esculenta 'Illustris,' a Proven Winners Selection (above), *C. esculenta* with coleus, ipomoea and others (right)

Elephant ears are often included in water gardens and can actually be grown in up to 20 cm (8") of water. Try them in a large water barrel if you want something other than miniature water lilies.

Also called: taro **Features:** tuberous; large, dark green to purple leaves **Height:** 60 cm–1.2 m (2–4') **Spread:** 60 cm–1.2 m (2–4') **Hardiness:** tender perennial grown as an annual

English Ivy
Hedera

H. helix with phormium and maidenhair vine

English ivy is a beautiful, versatile vine with dark, glossy, evergreen leaves that is well suited to both sun and shade.

Growing

English ivy prefers **light shade** or **partial shade** but will adapt to any light conditions from full sun to full shade. The potting mix should be **moist** and **well drained**. Fertilize every two weeks with quarter- to half-strength fertilizer. Although there are several hardy selections, the most decorative English ivy selections are not hardy in Canadian winters.

Tips

English ivy is a pretty, fast-growing vine. It quickly fills in the spaces between other plants in a mixed container or hanging basket and will trail over the edge of the pot.

Recommended

H. helix is a vigorous vine with glossy, dark green leaves. Many cultivars have been developed for outdoor cultivation, and they are often available in the vine section of your local garden centre. Many varieties of English ivy are grown as houseplants, and these are often the most interesting ones to include in your mixed containers. The following are just a few examples. **'Calico'** has green, grey and cream mottled foliage. **'Flamenco'** has small, frilly, dark green, glossy leaves. **'Maple Leaf'** has deeply lobed, star-like, dark green leaves.

Features: tender to hardy, evergreen or semi-evergreen climbing vine or groundcover; decorative foliage **Height:** 30 cm–3 m (1–10') in containers **Spread:** 30 cm–3 m (1–10') in containers **Hardiness:** zones 5–8; tender vine grown as an annual

Euonymus
Euonymus

E. fortunei GOLD SPLASH

Burning bush achieves the best fall colour when it is grown in full sun.

Features: deciduous or evergreen shrub, small tree, groundcover or climber; decorative foliage; good fall colour **Height:** 30 cm–3 m (1–10') in containers **Spread:** 30 cm–3 m (1–10') in containers **Hardiness:** zones 3–8

This group of variable shrubs includes some of the best-suited woody plants for container culture.

Growing

Euonymus prefers **full sun** but tolerates light shade or partial shade. The potting mix should be **moist** and **well drained**. Fertilize monthly with quarter-strength fertilizer. Move this plant to a sheltered location out of the wind and sun in winter.

Tips

Burning bush has a neat, rounded habit and works well as the centre plant in a large mixed container. Wintercreeper euonymus can be allowed to trail over the edge of a container, pruned to form a small shrub or trained to climb a small trellis. It can also be trained as a topiary plant.

Recommended

E. alatus (burning bush, winged euonymus) is an attractive, open, mounding, deciduous shrub. It grows far too large to be suitable for a container, but there are several dwarf selections that can be used. '**Compacta**' is a popular dwarf cultivar. It has dense, compact growth, reaching up to 3 m (10') tall and wide, though smaller with pruning and when grown in a container. FIRE BALL ('Select'), a Proven Winners Selection, is a hardier selection of 'Compacta' that grows up to 2.1 m (7') tall and wide. It has brilliant red fall colour.

E. fortunei (wintercreeper euonymus) as a species is rarely grown in favour of the wide and attractive variety of cultivars. These can be prostrate, climbing or mounding evergreens, often with attractive, variegated foliage. BLONDY ('Interbolwji') has yellow foliage with narrow, irregular, dark green margins. '**Coloratus**' (purpleleaf wintercreeper) has green foliage that turns red or purple in winter. '**Emerald Gaiety**' is a vigorous shrub that sends out long shoots that will attempt to scale any nearby surface. The foliage is bright green with irregular, creamy margins that turn pink in winter. '**Emerald 'n' Gold**' is a bushy selection that has green leaves with wide, gold margins. The foliage turns pinky red during winter and spring. (Zones 5–8)

E. alatus FIRE BALL (above)
E. fortunei 'Emerald 'n' Gold' (centre)

E. alatus (below)

Fan Flower

Scaevola

S. aemula with canna lily, verbena and others

Fan flower is native to Australia and Polynesia. Regular pinching and trimming will keep your fan flower bushy and blooming its best.

Features: decorative, bushy or trailing habit; blue, purple or white, fan-shaped flowers **Height:** 20–30 cm (8–12") **Spread:** up to 90 cm (36") or more **Hardiness:** tender perennial grown as an annual

Fan flower's intriguing, one-sided flowers add interest to hanging baskets, planters and window boxes.

Growing

Fan flower grows well in **full sun** or **light shade**. The potting mix should be **moist** and **well drained**. Water it regularly because this plant doesn't like to dry out completely. It does, however, recover quickly from wilting when watered. Fertilize every two weeks with quarter-strength fertilizer.

This plant is a perennial that is treated as an annual. Cuttings can be taken in late summer and grown indoors to be used the following summer.

Tips

Fan flower is popular for hanging baskets and as an edging plant in a container where it can trail down. It is also an attractive filler plant in mixed containers, as the trailing habit will spread between other plants.

Recommended

S. aemula forms a mound of foliage from which trailing stems emerge. The fan-shaped flowers come in shades of purple, usually with white bases. The species is rarely grown because there are many improved cultivars. 'Blue Wonder' has long, trailing branches, making it ideal for hanging baskets. It can eventually spread 90 cm (36") or more. 'Saphira' is a compact variety with deep blue flowers. WHIRLWIND BLUE is a compact plant that bears heat- and fade-resistant, blue flowers. WHIRLWIND WHITE bears white flowers on compact, heat-tolerant plants.

Fescue

Festuca

F. glauca ELIJAH BLUE with Swan River daisy and nemesia

This fine-leaved, ornamental grass forms tufted clumps that resemble pincushions.

Growing

Fescue grows well in **full sun** or **partial shade**. The potting mix should be **moist** and **well drained**. Fertilize once a month during the growing season with half-strength fertilizer. This grass is fairly drought tolerant, if you are prone to forgetting to water quite as often as you should. Move fescue containers to a sheltered location out of the wind and sun in winter.

Tips

Fescue is an interesting accent plant for mixed containers. It adds unusual texture and colour to annual and perennial combinations.

Recommended

F. filiformis (fine-leaf fescue) forms a low tuft of bright green, hair-like foliage.

It grows 15–20 cm (6–8") tall and spreads 20–30 cm (8–12").

F. glauca (blue fescue) forms tidy, tufted clumps of fine, blue-toned foliage and produces short spikes of flowers in early summer. Cultivars and hybrids come in varying heights and in shades ranging from blue to olive green. ELIJAH BLUE, a Proven Winners Selection, and **'Boulder Blue'** have intense blue colouring. **'Skinner's Blue'** is one of the hardiest selections, making it a good choice for container culture.

Trim plants back in spring before the new growth starts, and trim back the faded seedheads to keep your plants looking tidy.

Features: tuft-forming, perennial grass; silvery or grey-blue to olive green or bright green foliage; spiky or relaxed habit
Height: 15–30 cm (6–12") **Spread:** 25–30 cm (10–12") **Hardiness:** zones 3–8

Flowering Maple

Abutilon

A. x hybridum (above & below)

Flowering maple is a vigorous shrub with beautiful flowers and decorative foliage, and it deserves a place in both your garden and your house.

Growing

Flowering maple grows well in **full sun** or **light shade**. The potting mix should be **moist** and **well drained**. Fertilize every two weeks during the growing season with a quarter- to half-strength fertilizer. This tender plant must be moved indoors in winter if it is to survive. Trim it back annually to keep the size manageable.

Tips

Flowering maple makes a stunning specimen, but it is also a lovely companion plant. Plant mounding and trailing annuals around the base of flowering maple to create a pretty display for your front entryway.

Recommended

A. x *hybridum* (flowering maple) is a bushy shrub. It bears downy, maple-like leaves on woody branches. The single flowers are pendulous and bell shaped. There are a number of varieties available in a variety of colours including peach, white, cream, yellow, orange, red or pink. There are also several selections with variegated foliage. Some of the variegated selections bear very few flowers. **'Kentish Belle'** bears vibrant orange flowers. **'Nabob'** has crimson red flowers.

Features: pendulous flowers in shades of yellow, peach, orange, red, pink, cream or white; maple-like, sometimes variegated foliage **Height:** 1.2–1.5 m (4–5') **Spread:** 60–90 cm (24–36") **Hardiness:** tender shrub grown as an annual or overwintered indoors

Flowering maple is a long-lasting houseplant, providing years of enjoyment, and it will have denser growth with better foliage colour and more flowers if it spends every summer enjoying the great outdoors.

Fothergilla
Fothergilla

F. gardenii 'Blue Mist'

Fragrant flowers, stunning fall colour and interesting, brownish tan stems give fothergilla year-round appeal.

Growing

Fothergilla grows well in **full sun, light shade** or **partial shade**, though the best flowering and fall colour occurs in full sun. The potting mix should be **acidic, humus rich, moist** and **well drained**. Add compost or earthworm castings to the mix. Fertilize with quarter-strength fertilizer every two weeks during the growing season. Move containers to a sheltered location out of the wind and sun in winter.

Tips

Fothergilla forms a striking focal point in mixed containers. Combine it with spring-blooming plants like tulips for early season contrast and silver-leaved plants like dusty miller and licorice plant for fall contrast.

Recommended

F. gardenii (dwarf fothergilla) is a bushy shrub. The dark green leaves turn brilliant, mixed shades of yellow, orange and red in fall. Bottlebrush-shaped flowers are produced in spring and have a delicate honey fragrance. **'Blue Mist'** has blue-green foliage that is pretty in summer, but it doesn't develop brilliant fall colour like the species does.

F. major (large fothergilla) is very similar in appearance to dwarf fothergilla, but it is not as suitable for container culture because it grows at least twice as large.

Features: bushy shrub; attractive foliage; good fall colour; fragrant, white, spring flowers **Height:** 60–90 cm (24–36") **Spread:** 60–90 cm (24–36") **Hardiness:** zones 4–8

Fountain Grass

Pennisetum

P. glaucum 'Purple Majesty' with others

One beautiful feature of purple fountain grass is its foliage, which can be seen poking through the snow in winter.

Features: tender or semi-hardy, perennial grass; arching or upright habit; decorative foliage; fuzzy, pink, purple or tan, summer and fall flowers **Height:** 30 cm–1.8 m (1–6') **Spread:** 45 cm–1.2 m (18"–4') **Hardiness:** zones 5–8; tender perennial grown as an annual

Fountain grass is a low maintenance plant, even in a container, and it has a graceful, soft but also bold form that makes it a stunning companion in a mixed container.

Growing

Fountain grass grows best in **full sun**. The potting mix should be **well drained**. Fertilize monthly during the growing season with quarter-strength fertilizer. Some fountain grasses are grown as annuals and will have to be replaced each summer. Where they are hardy, perennial fountain grasses should be kept in a sheltered location out of the wind and sun where they will be protected from temperature fluctuations. Where they are not hardy, they can be cut back in fall and stored in a cool location indoors.

Tips

Fountain grass makes an interesting alternative to dracaena and spikes in mixed containers. The colourful foliage can be used to create colour-themed containers with perennials and annuals, whether you complement or contrast the colours. Textural contrast can be created if you combine fountain grass with ferns, ivies and sun-tolerant selections of hosta and coral bells.

Recommended

P. alopecuriodes forms clumps of long, narrow, bright green, arching leaves. Soft spikes of tan, pink or purple, fuzzy flowers are produced on long, arching stems in summer and fall. **'Hameln'** is a dwarf cultivar hardy to zone 5. **'Little Bunny'** is an even smaller selection that grows only 30 cm (12") tall.

P. glaucum **'Purple Majesty'** (purple majesty millet, ornamental millet) has a corn-like growth habit, with a strong central stalk and broad, blackish purple, strap-like leaves. The bottlebrush-like flower spikes are also purple, though the tiny flowers may be yellow.

P. setaceum **'Rubrum'** ('Purpureum,' annual fountain grass) is a dense, mound-forming, tender, perennial grass that is grown as an annual. It has narrow, dark purple foliage and large, showy, rose red flower spikes from midsummer to fall. BURGUNDY GIANT, a Proven Winners Selection, has wider, deep burgundy foliage. Its nodding flower spikes are pinkish purple.

P. setaceum BURGUNDY GIANT with spurge, mondo grass, coleus, english ivy and dwarf plumbago (above)
P. setaceum 'Rubrum' (below)

Geranium

Pelargonium

P. peltatum cultivar with lobelia

There are many scented-leaf geraniums available. Not only do they have fragrant foliage, but their foliage is often variegated and deeply lobed, sometimes even lacy-looking.

Features: decorative, often colourful foliage; red, pink, violet, orange, salmon, white or purple, summer flowers **Height:** 20–60 cm (8–24") **Spread:** 15 cm–1.2 m (6"–4') **Hardiness:** tender perennial grown as an annual

Geraniums are perhaps the quintessential container plant. Avoid the same old same old by selecting scented geraniums for their uniquely decorative and sometimes deliciously fragrant foliage as well as for their flowers.

Growing

Geraniums prefer **full sun** but tolerate partial shade, although they may not bloom as profusely. The potting mix should be **well drained**. Fertilize with quarter-strength fertilizer every one or two weeks during the growing season. Deadhead to keep geraniums blooming and looking neat, and pinch them back occasionally to keep plants bushy.

Geraniums are perennials that are treated as annuals. They can be kept indoors over winter in a bright room.

Tips
With their brightly coloured flowers and often decorative foliage, geraniums are very popular for mixed containers, window boxes and hanging baskets.

Recommended
P. capitatum is a compact plant with irregularly shaped, rose-scented leaves. It bears pinkish purple flowers.

P. '**Chocolate Peppermint**' has green leaves with irregular, bronze-purple centres. The flowers are pink and white. As the name suggests, the foliage smells like chocolatey peppermint.

P. crispum (lemon-scented geranium) forms a compact, low or upright mound of bright green, crinkly, lemon-scented foliage. It bears small, pink flowers in summer. '**Cream Peach**' has green, cream and yellow variegated, peach-scented foliage. '**Variegatum**' ('Variegated Prince Rupert') has ruffled, cream variegated, lemon-scented foliage.

P. peltatum (ivy-leaved geranium) has thick, waxy leaves and a trailing habit. It bears loose clusters of colourful flowers. Many cultivars are available.

P. zonale (zonal geranium) is a bushy plant with red, pink, purple, orange or white flowers and frequently banded or multi-coloured foliage. The **Fireworks Series** includes several cultivars with star-shaped flowers in several shades including red and pink. The maple leaf-shaped foliage is colourfully banded. Plants have a compact habit.

P. peltatum with portulaca in planter box and petunias (above), *P. peltatum* cultivar with jasmine and bacopa (below)

Glory Bush
Tibouchina

T. urvilleana

Glory bush is a wonderful, colourful accent plant that will give a tropical look to your containers.

Growing
Glory bush grows best in **full sun** in a sheltered location. The potting mix should be **slightly acidic, moist** and **well drained**. Fertilize every two weeks during the growing season with quarter- to half-strength fertilizer. This tender plant must be overwintered indoors in a sunny room.

Tips
Glory bush is useful as a specimen or as an accent in a mixed container. It can be trained into a small tree. The velvety leaves provide an attractive backdrop for red or orange flowers.

Recommended
T. urvilleana is a fast-growing, upright to rounded shrub. The dark green, velvety leaves may have red margins, and older foliage may be marked and spotted yellow, orange and red. Fat, rounded, red-tinged buds open to reveal vivid, royal purple flowers in late spring to late fall.

People in southeastern Brazil use the massed purple blooms to decorate churches at Easter time.

Also called: princess flower, pleroma, Brazilian spider flower **Features:** bushy, erect to rounded, evergreen shrub; purple flowers; dark green, velvety foliage **Height:** 1.5–3 m (5–10') **Spread:** 1.5–3 m (5–10') **Hardiness:** tender shrub grown as an annual or overwintered indoors

Hakone Grass

Hakonechloa

*H*akone grass is an attractive, shade-loving grass that provides interest throughout the growing season.

Growing

Hakone grass grows well in **light shade** or **partial shade**. The potting mix should be **moist** and **well drained**. Fertilize every two weeks during the growing season with quarter- to half-strength fertilizer. Where it is hardy, move containers to a sheltered location out of the wind and sun where it will be protected from temperature fluctuations in winter. Where it is not hardy, it can be cut back and overwintered in an unheated shed or garage.

Tips

Hakone grass is one of the few grasses that grows well in shaded locations. Its texture and colour are a good contrast to broad-leaved shade plants like hosta and lungwort. This grass creates a striking display spilling over the sides of containers.

Recommended

H. macra forms a clump of bright green, arching, grass-like foliage that turns deep pink in fall, then bronze as winter sets in. Several cultivars are available. **'All Gold'** has pure gold leaves and is more upright and spiky in habit. **'Aureola'** has bright yellow foliage with narrow, green streaks; the foliage turns pink in fall.

This ornamental grass is native to Japan, where it grows on mountainsides and cliffsides, often near streams and other water sources.

H. macra 'Aureola' with ligularia, begonia and lysimachia

Also called: Japanese forest grass
Features: perennial grass; arching habit; fall colour **Height:** 30–60 cm (12–24") **Spread:** 30–60 cm (12–24") **Hardiness:** zones 5–8

Hebe

Hebe

H. speciosa 'Tricolor'

Hebe is an attractive, tender shrub that can be included in Canadian gardens when it is grown in containers and moved indoors in winter.

Growing

Hebe grows well in **full sun, partial shade** or **light shade** in a sheltered location. The potting mix should be **neutral to alkaline, moist** and **well drained**. It grows in poor soil, so it only needs fertilizing once in early summer. This plant is not hardy in Canada and must be moved indoors in winter. Keep it in a cool, bright room. Hebe is tolerant of urban pollution.

Features: tender, mound-forming, evergreen shrub; dense, attractive foliage; purple, red, blue or white, fragrant flowers **Height:** 60 cm–1.5 m (2–5') **Spread:** 60 cm–1.5 m (2–5') **Hardiness:** zone 8; grown as an annual or overwintered indoors

Tips

Hebe can be used to create topiary specimens, which will add a whimsical touch to your container plantings. It can be mixed with annuals and perennials in mixed containers.

Recommended

H. **'Patty's Purple'** is a spreading, mounding shrub with wine red stems, densely covered with small, dark green, glossy leaves. It bears clusters of purple flowers in spring and summer. The flowers fade to white with age.

H. speciosa is a stout shrub with thick branches and large, shiny, dark green leaves. It bears red-purple to blue-purple flowers in summer.

H. **'Veronica Lake'** is a compact, mounding shrub that bears clusters of lilac purple flowers in summer.

Heliotrope

Heliotropium

Heliotrope's big clusters of fragrant flowers on bushy plants have renewed the popularity of this old-fashioned favourite.

Growing

Heliotrope grows best in **full sun**. The potting mix should be **humus rich, moist** and **well drained**. Fertilize once a month during the growing season with quarter-strength fertilizer. Plants can be treated as houseplants in winter; keep them in a cool and sunny location indoors.

Tips

Heliotrope is ideal for growing in containers placed where the wonderful scent of the flowers can be enjoyed. Combine purple-flowered heliotrope with yellow- or white-flowered plants and plants with burgundy foliage for striking colour contrasts.

Recommended

H. arborescens is a low, bushy shrub that is treated like an annual. It bears large clusters of sweet-scented, purple flowers all summer. Some new cultivars are not as strongly scented as the species. 'Alba' is a compact plant that has white flower clusters. ATLANTIS, a Proven Winners Selection, bears large, fragrant clusters of royal purple flowers. 'Black Beauty' bears deep purple, fragrant flowers.

These old-fashioned flowers may have been popular in your grandmother's garden. Their recent comeback is no surprise, considering their attractive foliage, flowers and scent.

H. arborescens ATLANTIS with angelonia, lobelia, sweet flag, licorice plant and sage

Also called: cherry pie plant **Features:** bushy habit; purple or white, fragrant flowers; attractive foliage **Height:** 20–60 cm (8–24") **Spread:** 30–60 cm (12–24") **Hardiness:** tender shrub grown as an annual or over-wintered indoors

Hens and Chicks

Sempervivum

S. tectorum with phormium

These curious plants can grow on almost any surface. In the past they were grown on tile roofs—it was believed they would protect the house from lightning.

Also called: houseleek **Features:** rosette-forming, succulent perennial; red, yellow, white or purple flowers **Height:** 5–15 cm (2–6") **Spread:** 30 cm (12") or more **Hardiness:** zones 3–8

Hens and chicks are easy to grow. They need little care other than a very well-drained soil and a light sprinkle of water during extended dry periods.

Growing

Hens and chicks grow well in **full sun** or **partial shade**. The potting mix should be very **well drained**. Add fine gravel or grit to the mix to provide adequate drainage. Fertilize once or twice during the growing season with quarter-strength fertilizer.

Tips

These plants can be used in shallow troughs and make interesting centrepieces on patio and picnic tables. They can also be combined with other drought-tolerant plants, like sedum and yarrow, in mixed containers.

Recommended

S. tectorum is one of the most commonly grown hens and chicks. It forms a low-growing mat of fleshy-leaved rosettes. Small, new rosettes are quickly produced and grow and multiply to fill almost any space. Flowers may be produced in summer but are not common in Canadian gardens. **'Atropurpureum'** has dark reddish purple leaves. **'Limelight'** has yellow-green, pink-tipped foliage. **'Pacific Hawk'** has dark red leaves that are edged with silvery hairs.

S. arachnoideum (cobweb houseleek) is identical to *S. tectorum* except that the tips of the leaves are entwined with hairy fibres, giving the appearance of cobwebs. This plant may need protection during wet weather.

Holly

Ilex

I. verticillata 'Sparkleberry'

The cold winters experienced in many Canadian gardens limit the number of hollies we can grow in our gardens, but you'll be surprised by how many will grow quite happily in a container.

Growing

Holly prefers **full sun** but tolerates partial shade and likes a sheltered location where it is protected from drying winds. The potting mix should be **humus rich**

All hollies have male and female flowers on separate plants, and both must be present for the females to set fruit. One male plant will adequately pollinate two or three females.

Features: erect or spreading, evergreen or deciduous shrub; spiny, glossy, dark green foliage; red, orange or yellow fruit **Height:** 90 cm–3 m (3–10') **Spread:** 90 cm–2.4 m (3–8') **Hardiness:** zones 3–8

I. x meserveae 'Golden Girl' (above)
I. verticillata 'Spravey' (below)

and **moist**. Mix in compost or earthworm castings. Fertilize once a month during the growing season. Where shrubs aren't hardy in winter, move containers to a sheltered location protected from sun and wind or into a garage or shed where they will be protected from extremes of temperature.

Tips

Hollies make interesting additions to containers. Their glossy foliage provides an attractive background for brightly coloured annuals. Their fruit is decorative, especially in winter, and adds a pretty accent to your sheltered patio or balcony.

Recommended

I. glabra (inkberry) is a rounded shrub with glossy, deep green, evergreen foliage and dark purple fruit. It is rather large to include in a container garden, but several suitable dwarf cultivars that grow up to 90 cm (36") are available. **'Compacta'** is a female dwarf cultivar with a dense, branching habit. **'Nigra'** is a female dwarf cultivar with dark, glossy leaves. The foliage develops a purple hue in winter. (Zones 4–8)

I. x meserveae (blue holly) is an erect or spreading, dense, evergreen shrub that bears glossy, red fruit that persists into winter. Tolerant of pruning, it can be trimmed to keep it to a reasonable size. Many cultivars have been developed, including several suitable dwarf selections. (Zones 5–8)

I. verticillata (winterberry, winterberry holly) is a deciduous species grown for its explosion of red fruit that persists into winter. It grows 1.8–2.4 m (6–8') tall, with an equal spread. It is a bit large for container culture, but it is the hardiest species. Cultivars, including dwarf selections, are available. **'Red Sprite'** is a dwarf cultivar that bears bright red fruit.

Hosta
Hosta

H. cultivar with others

There are almost endless variations in hosta foliage; swirls, stripes, puckers and ribs enhance the leaves' various sizes, shapes and colours.

Hosta leaves can be used in fresh flower arrangements.

Growing

Hostas prefer **light shade** or **partial shade** but will grow in full shade. Some will tolerate full sun. The potting mix should be **moist** and **well drained**. Fertilize plants monthly during the growing season with half-strength fertilizer.

Features: clump-forming perennial; decorative foliage in shades of green or variegated with yellow or cream; late-summer or fall, mauve, purple or white flowers **Height:** 30 cm–1.2 m (1–4') **Spread:** 45–90 cm (18–36") **Hardiness:** zones 3–8

H. fortuneii 'Francee' (above), *H.* cultivar (centre)

H. cultivar with coral bells and barberry (below)

Move containers to a sheltered location in winter.

Tips

Hostas are wonderful woodland plants and look very attractive when combined with ferns and other fine-textured plants. Combine a variety of hostas together or mix them with other plants.

Recommended

Hostas have been subjected to a great deal of crossbreeding and hybridizing, resulting in hundreds of cultivars. The following are just a few of the possibilities. **'Baby Bunting'** is a popular cultivar with dark green to slightly bluish green, heart-shaped leaves and light purple flowers. **'Fragrant Bouquet'** has bright green leaves with creamy yellow margins and very fragrant, white flowers. **'Gold Standard'** is a hosta fancier's favourite, bearing bright yellow leaves with narrow, green margins. **'Guacamole'** has chartreuse leaves with dark green margins and fragrant, white flowers. **'June'** has bright yellow leaves with blue-green margins and light purple flowers. **'Pandora's Box'** forms a compact mound of creamy leaves with irregular, green margins and bears light purple flowers. **'Tardiflora'** forms an attractive, small mound of dark green leaves and bears lots of light purple flowers in fall.

Choosing containers that are proportionate to the mature size of your hostas is of prime importance if you're planning on overwintering them for more than a year. It's wise to learn the mature size of the hosta, then select your container based on that information.

Hydrangea
Hydrangea

Proven Winners Selection *H. paniculata* LIMELIGHT

From rounded shrubs and small trees to climbing vines, hydrangeas offer a wealth of possibilities for use in containers.

Growing

Hydrangeas grow well in **full sun** or **partial shade**, and some species tolerate full shade. These plants perform best in cool, moist conditions, and some shade will reduce leaf and flower scorch in hotter gardens. The potting mix should

Try an Annabelle hydrangea with white-flowering daylilies and hostas and a silver-leaved lamium to create a beautiful, white garden in a shady corner.

Features: mounding, spreading or climbing, deciduous shrub or tree; clusters of white, pink, blue, purple or red flowers in summer; attractive foliage, sometimes with good fall colour; some with exfoliating bark **Height:** 90 cm–3 m (3–10') **Spread:** 90 cm–3 m (3–10') **Hardiness:** zones 3–8

H. macrophylla (above & below)

be **humus rich, moist** and **well drained**. Fertilize monthly during the growing season with quarter- to half-strength fertilizer. Move containers to a sheltered location out of the wind and sun in winter.

Tips

Hydrangeas can really brighten up your mixed containers with their large flower clusters. Shrubby forms can be grown alone or combined with other plants. Tree forms are small enough to grow in containers but large enough to offer a good vertical accent. Climbing hydrangea can be grown in a large container and used to create a beautiful display against a wall or even over the edge of a balcony.

Recommended

H. anomala subsp. *petiolaris* (climbing hydrangea) is an elegant climbing plant with dark green, glossy leaves. It bears clusters of lacy-looking flowers in mid-summer. (Zones 4–8)

H. arborescens 'Annabelle' (Annabelle hydrangea) is a rounded shrub that bears large clusters of white flowers, even in shady conditions.

H. macrophylla (bigleaf hydrangea) is a rounded shrub that bears flowers in shades of white, pink, red, blue or purple from mid- to late summer. Many cultivars are available. (Zones 5–8)

H. paniculata 'Grandiflora' (Peegee hydrangea) is a spreading to upright large shrub or small tree that bears white flowers from late summer to early fall. (Zones 4–8)

H. quercifolia (oakleaf hydrangea) is a mound-forming shrub with attractive, cinnamon brown, exfoliating bark. Its large leaves are lobed like an oak's and turn bronze to bright red in fall. It bears conical clusters of sterile as well as fertile flowers. (Zones 4–8)

Hyssop
Agastache

This perennial is a favourite with hummingbirds, butterflies and other pollinators.

Growing

Hyssop grows well in **full sun** or **partial shade**. The potting mix should be **well drained**. Fertilize every two weeks during the growing season with quarter-strength fertilizer. Deadheading will keep plants neat and encourage continued blooming. Tender selections will have to be overwintered indoors or replaced each year. Hardy selections can be kept in a sheltered spot outdoors in winter.

Tips

These bushy plants make good companions in mixed containers. Combine them with lavender, scented-leaf geranium, lilac and thyme for a fragrance-themed container that is sure to attract pollinators to your garden.

Recommended

A. aurantiaca is a bushy, upright plant with grey-green, mint-scented leaves. It bears spikes of orange-pink flowers in summer. 'Apricot Sprite' bears lots of apricot orange flowers. (Zones 7–8)

A. 'Firebird' has irregular, bronzy maroon markings on its leaves and bears spikes of coppery orange flowers in summer. (Zones 6–8)

A. foeniculum (anise hyssop) is a bushy, upright, anise-scented perennial with slightly downy leaves and dense spikes of lilac blue flowers. 'Snow Spike' has white flowers.

A. foeniculum

The leaves of anise hyssop can be diffused in hot water for tea.

Features: bushy, upright, tender or hardy perennial; mint- or licorice-scented foliage; pink, purple, purple-blue or orange flowers **Height:** 30–90 cm (12–36") **Spread:** 30–90 cm (12–36") **Hardiness:** zones 2–8; tender perennial grown as an annual

Impatiens
Impatiens

I. walleriana with ageratum and vinca

mpatiens, with their brightly coloured flowers, are just as valuable in shady containers as they are in ground-based gardens.

Growing

Impatiens do best in **partial shade** or **light shade** but tolerate full shade or, if kept moist, full sun. New Guinea impatiens are best adapted to sunny locations. The potting mix should be **humus rich, moist** and **well drained**. Mix in some compost or earthworm castings. Fertilize every two weeks during the growing season with quarter-strength fertilizer.

Tips

These bushy or spreading plants make a great colourful filler in shady containers. Choose impatiens for the contrast or complement their flowers can create with the other plants in your containers.

Recommended

I. hawkeri **New Guinea Group** (New Guinea impatiens) are bushy plants with glossy, dark green foliage that is often variegated with a yellow stripe down the centre. The flowers come in shades of red, orange, pink, purple or white. Cultivars are available.

I. walleriana (busy Lizzie) is a bushy, spreading plant with glossy leaves in shades of light through dark green or bronze. The flowers come in shades of purple, red, burgundy, pink, orange, salmon, apricot, yellow, white or bicoloured. Many cultivars are available.

The name Impatiens *refers to the impatient nature of the seedpods. When ripe, the seedpods burst open with the slightest touch and scatter their seeds.*

Features: bushy or spreading habit; flowers in shades of purple, red, burgundy, pink, orange, salmon, apricot, yellow or white, or bicoloured
Height: 15–45 cm (6–18")
Spread: 20–60 cm (8–24")
Hardiness: tender annual

Ipomoea

Ipomoea

I. batatas BLACK HEART, from Proven Winners

Agroup of vigorous vines looks stunning spilling over the edges of mixed containers.

Growing

Ipomoeas grow well in **full sun**. The potting mix should be **light** and **well drained**. Fertilize sweet potato vine once a month with quarter- to half-strength fertilizer during the growing season. Other ipomoeas will bloom poorly if over-fertilized.

Grow moonflower on a porch or on a trellis near a patio that is used in the evenings so that the sweetly scented flowers can be fully enjoyed.

Features: twining climber; white, blue, pink or purple flowers; sometimes variegated or colourful foliage **Height:** 30 cm–3 m (1–10') **Spread:** 30–60 cm (12–24") **Hardiness:** annual; tender perennial grown as an annual

I. batatas 'Margarita' with coleus, english ivy, lamium and others (above), *I. batatas* 'Margarita' with juniper, coral bells and bamboo grass (below)

Tips

Ipomoeas make excellent filler and accent plants in planters and hanging baskets. Sweet potato vines have colourful foliage, and morning glories and moonflowers have lovely, trumpet-shaped flowers. The climbing vines will grow up small trellises or other structures.

Recommended

I. alba (moonflower) is a twining, perennial climber with heart-shaped leaves and sweetly scented, white flowers that open only at night.

I. batatas (sweet potato vine) is a twining, perennial climber that is usually treated as a bushy or trailing plant rather than a climber. It is grown for its attractive foliage rather than its flowers. Cultivars with different foliage colour variations are available. **'Blackie'** has dark purple (almost black), deeply lobed leaves. **'Terrace Lime'** ('Margarita') has yellow-green foliage on a fairly compact plant. **'Tricolor'** is a compact plant with light green, cream and bright pink variegated leaves.

I. purpurea (morning glory) is a twining, annual climber with heart-shaped leaves and trumpet-shaped, purple, pink, blue or white flowers.

I. tricolor (morning glory) is a twining, annual climber with heart-shaped, purple or blue flowers with white throats. There are several cultivars, including the popular **'Heavenly Blue,'** which has sky blue flowers with white centres.

Iris

Iris

*I*rises are valuable both for their strap-like foliage and their beautiful, colourful flowers.

Growing

Irises grow best in **full sun** but tolerate partial shade or light shade. The potting mix should be **moist** and **well drained**, though several species are tolerant of dry conditions. Fertilize monthly during the growing season with quarter-strength fertilizer. Move containers to a sheltered location out of the wind and sun in winter.

Tips

Irises provide a wonderful strong, vertical accent. Several species grow in wet soil and can be combined with other moisture-lovers like monkey flower and elephant ears for a bog-themed container. There are iris flowers in almost every imaginable shade, and these can be used to create complementary or contrasting combinations in mixed containers.

Recommended

I. ensata (Japanese iris) is a water-loving species that bears blue, purple, pink or white flowers in early to mid-summer.

I. germanica hybrids (German iris, bearded iris) are drought-tolerant plants that bear the most decorative flowers in every imaginable colour.

I. pallida (sweet iris, variegated iris) is a drought-tolerant, purple-flowered species that is rarely grown, but its variegated cultivars are a useful addition to mixed containers. '**Argentea Variegata**' has cream-and-green-striped foliage. '**Aurea Variegata**' has yellow-and-green-striped foliage.

Iris with others

Features: clump-forming, rhizomatous perennial; narrow or broad, strap-like, possibly variegated foliage; summer flowers in every shade of the rainbow **Height:** 30 cm–1.2 m (1–4') **Spread:** 20–90 cm (8–36") **Hardiness:** zones 2–8

I. pseudacorus (yellow flag iris) is a moisture-loving species with narrow foliage and bright yellow, brown- or purple-marked flowers in mid- and late summer.

I. siberica (Siberian iris) likes a moist but well-drained soil. It bears purple flowers in early summer, though cultivars with pink, blue, white, yellow or red flowers are available.

I. versicolor (blue flag iris) is a moisture-loving species that bears flowers in varied shades of purple in early summer.

Irises are steeped in history and lore. The name Iris *comes from the Greek messenger to the gods, who travelled using the rainbow as a bridge.*

I. germanica 'Stepping Out' (above), *I. pseudacorus* (below)

Kalanchoe
Kalanchoe

K. blossfeldiana

Kalanchoe is an extremely varied group of plants. There are fuzzy ones, waxy ones, cascading ones and upright ones; some have decorative foliage, others are grown strictly for flowers.

Growing
Kalanchoes grow best in **light shade** or **partial shade** with protection from the hot afternoon sun. The potting mix should be **well drained**. Fertilize monthly with half-strength fertilizer during the growing season. Plants can be moved indoors and treated as houseplants at the end of summer.

Tips
Kalanchoes are interesting accent plants that add a touch of the unusual to your mixed containers. Their drought tolerance makes them useful for gardeners who occasionally forget to water.

Recommended
K. blossfeldiana (flaming katy) is a bushy, upright plant with rounded, fleshy leaves with scalloped edges. The flowers are borne in large clusters in colours such as yellow, peach, red, white or pink.

K. tomentosa (panda plant, pussy ears) is a bushy, upright plant with grey-green leaves that are covered in short, silvery hairs. The tips and margins are marked with brown.

Once sold as a seasonal holiday flowering plant, flaming katy is now available year round, though it is still sold as Christmas kalanchoe.

Features: colourful flowers; glossy or fuzzy foliage **Height:** 15–45 cm (6–18") **Spread:** 25–45 cm (10–18") **Hardiness:** tender perennial grown as an annual

Lady's Mantle
Alchemilla

A. mollis

The chartreuse yellow flower sprays make interesting substitutes for baby's breath in fresh and dried arrangements.

Features: mound-forming perennial; yellow or yellow-green, summer and early-fall flowers; attractive, downy foliage **Height:** 5–45 cm (2–18") **Spread:** 45–60 cm (18–24") **Hardiness:** zones 3–8

*F*ew other perennials look as captivating as lady's mantle does with droplets of morning dew clinging like shimmering pearls to its velvety leaves.

Growing

Lady's mantle grows well in **light shade** or **partial shade** with protection from the afternoon sun. Hot locations and excessive sun will scorch the leaves. The potting mix should be **humus rich, moist** and **well drained**. Fertilize every two weeks during the growing season with quarter-strength fertilizer. Leaves can be sheared back in summer if they begin to look tired and heat stressed; new leaves will emerge. Move containers to a sheltered location where they will be protected from temperature fluctuations in winter.

Tips

Lady's mantle is ideal for mixed containers, where it has a visually softening effect. Combine it with yellow- and purple-flowered annuals for an elegant, contrasting combination.

Recommended

A. alpina (alpine lady's mantle) is a low-growing plant that reaches 8–12 cm (3–5") in height and spreads about 50 cm (20"). Clusters of tiny, yellow flowers are borne in summer.

A. mollis (common lady's mantle) forms a mound of soft, rounded foliage and produces sprays of frothy-looking, yellowish green flowers in early summer. It grows 20–45 cm (8–18") tall and spreads about 60 cm (24").

Lamium

Lamium

L. maculatum 'White Nancy,' a Proven Winners Selection, with others

These plants, with their striped, dotted or banded, silver and green foliage provide a summer-long attraction and thrive on the barest neccessities of life.

Lamium is usually quite invasive in the ground. Growing it in containers keeps it from spreading out of control.

Growing

Lamium grows well in **light shade** or **partial shade** with protection from the hot afternoon sun. The potting mix should be **moist** and **well drained**. Fertilize no more than once a month with

Features: spreading or trailing perennial; decorative, variegated foliage; pink, white, yellow or purple, small, summer flowers **Height:** 15–30 cm (6–12") **Spread:** 30–60 cm (12–24") **Hardiness:** zones 2–8

L. galeobdolon 'Florentium' with others (above)
L. maculatum 'Beacon Silver' with impatiens (below)

quarter-strength fertilizer. Move containers to a sheltered location in winter where they will be protected from temperature fluctuations.

Tips

Lamium is a stunning foliage plant, and its spreading nature makes it a fantastic filler plant in mixed containers. It will trail over the edges of containers and hanging baskets.

Recommended

L. galeobdolon (*Lamiastrum galeobdolon*; yellow archangel, false lamium) is a mounding, spreading plant with silver-marked leaves and short spikes of yellow flowers in summer. **'Florentium'** ('Variegatum') is a low-growing cultivar with silvery leaves edged in green. **'Hermann's Pride'** forms a dense mat of white-speckled leaves. **'Silver Angel'** is a spreading plant with silvery foliage. (Zones 3–8)

L. maculatum (spotted dead nettle) is a low-growing, spreading plant with green leaves with white or silvery markings. It bears short spikes of pink, white or mauve flowers in summer. **'Anne Greenaway'** has silver, green and yellow variegated leaves and lavender flowers. **'Aureum'** has variegated chartreuse and silver foliage and pink flowers. **'Beacon Silver'** has silvery leaves with dark green margins and pink flowers. **'Orchid Frost'** has silvery foliage edged in blue-green and bears deep pink blooms. **'White Nancy'** has silvery white foliage and white flowers.

Lavender

Lavandula

Lavender is a beautiful, aromatic plant that is a welcome addition to sunny container gardens.

Growing

Lavender grows best in **full sun**. The potting mix should be **alkaline** and **well drained**. Once established, this plant tolerates heat and drought. Fertilize monthly during the growing season with quarter-strength fertilizer. Move containers to a sheltered location and cover them, or move them to an unheated shed or garage to protect them, in winter.

Tips

Lavender is a wonderful, aromatic plant that makes a good shrubby addition to mixed containers. Good companions for this plant include other drought-tolerant specimens, such as pinks, thyme and sedum.

Recommended

L. angustifolia (English lavender) is an aromatic, bushy shrub often treated as a perennial. From mid-summer to fall, it bears spikes of small flowers in varied shades of purple. **'Hidcote'** ('Hidcote Blue') bears spikes of deep purple flowers. **'Jean Davis'** is a compact cultivar with spikes of pale pink flowers. **'Lady'** bears purple flowers and can be grown from seed to flower the first summer.

L. x *intermedia* is a rounded shrub with aromatic, grey-green leaves and spikes of blue or purple flowers held on long stems.

L. stoechas (French lavender) is a compact, bushy shrub with grey-green leaves and dark purple flower spikes. (Zone 8)

L. angustifolia

The relaxing, soothing scent of lavender is often used in aromatherapy. Dry a few sprigs to use in sachets and pillows or in the bath.

Features: bushy, woody shrub; narrow, grey-green leaves; purple, pink or blue, mid-summer to fall flowers **Height:** 20–60 cm (8–24")
Spread: 30–60 cm (12–24")
Hardiness: zones 5–8

Leymus

Leymus

Leymus is a tough, colourful, tolerant grass that is a great plant for use
in container gardens.

Growing

Leymus grows best in **full sun**. The potting mix should be **moist** and **well
drained**. Leymus will tolerate partial to
light shade and both wet and dry situations. Fertilize monthly during the
growing season with quarter-strength
fertilizer. Move it to a sheltered location
in winter, or store it in a shed or garage
where it is not hardy.

Tips

The tall, blue-green, linear foliage of
leymus adds wonderful contrasting
colour and texture to mixed containers.

Recommended

L. arenarius is an upright, perennial
grass that forms clumps of blue-green,
arching foliage. Its spikes of blue-green
flowers can reach 1.5 m (5') tall in summer. The flower spikes fade to tan by
fall.

*Even though leymus spreads somewhat
aggressively by rhizomes in sandy soils, it
is fairly easy to keep it under control in
clay soils.*

L. arenarius

Also called: blue lyme grass **Features:**
attractive foliage **Height:** 60–90 cm (24–36")
Spread: 60–90 cm (24–36")
Hardiness: zones 4–8

Licorice Plant

Helichrysum

H. petiolare 'Petite Licorice' with dusty miller

The silvery sheen of licorice plant, caused by a fine, soft pubescence on its leaves, makes it a perfect complement for many other plants.

Growing

Licorice plant prefers **full sun**. The potting mix should be **neutral to alkaline** and **well drained**. Licorice plant wilts if the soil dries out but revives quickly once watered. It is easy to start more plants from cuttings in fall, giving you a supply of new plants for the following spring. Once they have rooted, keep the young plants in a cool, bright room during winter.

Tips

Include licorice plant in your hanging baskets and container plantings, and the trailing growth will quickly fill in and provide a soft, silvery backdrop for the colourful flowers of other plants as it cascades over the edges.

Recommended

H. petiolare is a trailing plant with fuzzy, grey-green leaves. The cultivars are more common than the species. **'Crispum'** has small leaves with rippled edges. **'Lemon Licorice'** has yellow-green foliage. **'Licorice Splash'** has grey-green leaves with irregular, creamy margins. **'Limelight'** has bright lime green leaves. **'Petite Licorice'** is a compact selection with small, grey-green leaves. **'Silver'** has grey-green leaves covered in a silvery white down. **'White Licorice'** has silvery white foliage.

Features: tender, bushy or trailing shrub or perennial; downy, grey-green, silvery, yellow or cream and green variegated foliage
Height: 15–60 cm (6–24") **Spread:** 30 cm–1.2 m (1–4') **Hardiness:** tender perennial grown as an annual

Lilac

Syringa

S. x *hyacinthiflora* 'Maiden's Blush'

Lilacs are frost-loving shrubs that don't flower at all in the warm southern climates.

Features: rounded or suckering, deciduous shrub or small tree with attractive, late-spring to mid-summer flowers **Height:** 90 cm–6 m (3–20') **Spread:** 90 cm–6 m (3–20') **Hardiness:** zones 3–8

Even for container gardeners, the hardest thing about growing lilacs is choosing from the many species and hundreds of cultivars available.

Growing

Lilacs grow best in **full sun**. The potting mix should be **humus rich** and **well drained.** Fertilize monthly with quarter-strength fertilizer. Lilacs are among the hardiest of plants. Move containers to a location out of the sun and wind, and they should make it through just about anything a Canadian winter can throw at them.

Tips

Lilacs make lovely vertical accents and are good structural plants for large containers. Most can be trained into a tree form and can be grown in a container for several years before they become too large and need to be transplanted into a garden.

Recommended

S. x *hyacinthiflora* (hyacinth-flowered lilac, early-flowering lilac) is a group of hardy, upright hybrids that become spreading as they mature. Clusters of fragrant flowers appear two weeks earlier than those of French lilacs. The leaves turn reddish purple in fall. Many excellent, disease-resistant cultivars are available.

S. meyeri (Meyer lilac) is a compact, rounded shrub that bears pink or lavender, fragrant flowers. **'Palibin'** (Palibin lilac) is a slow-growing cultivar with pinkish purple flowers. **'Tinkerbelle'** bears deep pink flowers.

S. patula **'Miss Kim'** is a dwarf, compact lilac with pale purple flower buds that open lavender blue. It has attractive, dark green foliage and vigorous growth.

S. reticulata (Japanese tree lilac) is a rounded, large shrub or small tree that bears white flowers. **'Ivory Silk'** has a more compact habit and produces more flowers than the species. This species and its cultivar are large plants for container culture. They can grow to over 3 m (10') tall, so be sure you have enough space for them to grow into. A small balcony will not accommodate the spread of these plants, but a large terrace or patio will.

S. x *hyacinthiflora* 'Evangeline' (above)
S. meyeri 'Palibin' (below)

Lilyturf
Liriope

L. muscari 'Monroe White'

These plants are heat-tolerant, making them popular where summer temperatures are frequently high, and plants that stay green and attractive with minimal care are much appreciated.

Resistant to drought, heat, humidity and most pests and diseases, lilyturf is one tough plant.

Growing
Lilyturf grows best in **light shade** or **partial shade** but tolerates both full sun and full shade well. The potting mix should be **humus rich, acidic, moist** and **well drained**. Fertilize monthly during the growing season with quarter-strength fertilizer. Where they are not hardy, plants will have to be stored in a shed or garage in winter or treated like annuals and replaced in spring.

Tips
Lilyturf is a good choice as a sort of container groundcover in warm Canadian gardens. If you have containers of shrubs and trees that you don't want to replant with annuals every year, lilyturf will form a low, dense mat of narrow, arching foliage with spikes of blue, purple or white flowers. It also makes an attractive addition to a mixed container.

Recommended
L. muscari forms a mass of low clumps of strap-like, evergreen leaves. It bears spikes of purple flowers from late summer through fall. **'Big Blue'** bears large spikes of purple-blue flowers. **'Monroe White'** bears white flowers. **'Pee Dee Gold Ingot'** has golden yellow to chartreuse leaves that mature to a bright yellow. It bears light purple flowers. **'Variegata'** has green-and-white-striped leaves and bears purple flowers.

Features: clump-forming, evergreen perennial; narrow, grass-like, dark green foliage; spikes of blue, purple or white, fall flowers **Height:** 20–45 cm (8–18") **Spread:** 45 cm (18") **Hardiness:** zones 6–8

Lobelia

Lobelia

L. *erinus* cultivars and others (above)
L. *erinus* (below)

Both the annual and perennial selections of lobelia are interesting to use in container gardens. Each adds a unique touch.

Growing

Lobelia grows well in **full sun** or **partial shade**, with partial or light shade preferable for annual lobelia in the hot and humid parts of Canada. The potting mix should be **humus rich, moist** and fairly **well drained**. Cardinal flower tolerates wet soil. Fertilize every two to four weeks with quarter-strength fertilizer. Cardinal flower should be moved to a sheltered location, preferably an unheated garage, in winter.

Features: bushy to upright perennial or annual; purple, blue, pink, white or red, summer to fall flowers **Height:** 10–60 cm (4–24") **Spread:** 15 cm (6") or more **Hardiness:** zones 4–8; annual

L. erinus 'Sapphire' with lamium and impatiens (above)
L. cardinalis (below)

Tips

Use annual lobelia in mixed containers or hanging baskets. The delicate, airy appearance adds a glaze of colour that looks particularly attractive with broad-leaved plants like hosta and lady's mantle.

Cardinal flower has a more upright habit, and its often bronzy foliage gives mixed containers an elegant appearance. Its ability to grow in moist to wet soil makes it suitable for boggy containers with other moisture lovers.

Recommended

L. cardinalis (cardinal flower) forms an upright clump of bronzy green foliage. It bears spikes of bright red flowers in summer and fall.

L. erinus may be rounded and bushy or low and trailing. It bears flowers in shades of blue, purple, red, pink or white. **Laguna Series** has heat-resisitant, trailing plants with flowers in a variety of colours. **Riviera Series** has flowers in shades of blue and purple on compact, bushy plants.

L. x speciosa (hybrid cardinal flower) is a vigorous, bushy plant. Hardiness varies from hybrid to hybrid. It bears flowers in shades of red, blue, purple, pink or white in summer and fall.

Trim annual lobelia back after the first wave of flowers. It will stop blooming in the hottest part of summer but usually revives in fall.

Lotus Vine

Lotus

*D*on't plant lotus vine solely for the flowers, as this annual is highly sought after for its unique, ferny foliage and bushy but trailing growth habit, making it perfectly suited to planter boxes and decorative containers.

Growing

Lotus vine grows well in **full sun** or **partial shade**. The potting mix should be **well drained**. This annual can tolerate hot and dry locations. Pinch the new tips back in late spring or early summer to promote bushier growth. Fertilize monthly with quarter-strength fertilizer.

Tips

Lotus vine is often grown in containers of all shapes and sizes. Its cascading habit and striking, unique foliage is most effective when allowed to trail over the side of a decorative pot, window box or built-in planter. The flowers are bright and colourful, and they contrast with the silvery green, ferny foliage. Lotus vine complements purple- and yellow-flowering annuals and chartreuse- or bronze-leaved foliage plants.

Recommended

L. berthelotii is a trailing plant with silvery stems covered in fine, soft, needle-like foliage. Small clusters of vivid orange to scarlet flowers that resemble lobster claws are borne in spring and summer.

L. hirsutus is a bushy or trailing perennial with fine, grey-green foliage. It bears pink-flushed, white flowers in summer and fall.

L. x **'Amazon Sunset'** has grey-green, needle-like foliage and vibrantly hued yellow-orange flowers that darken toward the edge.

L. berthelotii with pansies

Lotus vine is also commonly known as parrot's beak, coral gem, pelican's beak and double bird's foot trefoil, names that usually refer to the flowers' appearance.

Features: bushy or trailing habit; orange, red or yellow, summer through fall flowers
Height: 15–20 cm (6–8") **Spread:** 90 cm (36") or more **Hardiness:** tender perennial grown as an annual

Lungwort

Pulmonaria

P. GAELIC SUNSET with impatiens and wishbone flower

The wide array of lungworts have highly attractive foliage that ranges in colour from apple green to silver-spotted and olive to dark emerald green.

Growing

Lungworts prefer **partial to full shade**. The potting mix should be **humus rich, moist** and **well drained**. Mix in compost or earthworm castings. Fertilize monthly with half-strength fertilizer during the growing season. Move plants to a sheltered location in winter.

Features: clump-forming perennial; decorative, mottled foliage; blue, red, pink or white, spring flowers **Height:** 20–60 cm (8–24") **Spread:** 20–60 cm (8–24") **Hardiness:** zones 3–8

Tips

Lungworts are useful, attractive plants for shady and woodland-themed containers. Their foliage complements and contrasts with brightly coloured flowers.

Recommended

P. longifolia (long-leaved lungwort) forms a dense clump of long, narrow, white-spotted, green leaves and bears clusters of blue flowers. Cultivars are available.

P. officinalis (common lungwort, spotted dog) forms a loose clump of white-spotted, evergreen foliage. The flowers open pink and mature to blue. Cultivars are available.

P. saccharata (Bethlehem sage) forms a compact clump of large, white-spotted, evergreen leaves and purple, red or white flowers. Many cultivars and hybrids with other lungwort species are available.

Lysimachia
Lysimachia

These vigorous, carefree plants will enjoy a spot in a moist bog-themed container planting.

Growing

Lysimachia grows well in **full sun** or **partial shade**. The potting mix should be **moist** and **well drained**, though this plant is tolerant of wet soil. Fertilize monthly with quarter- to half-strength fertlizer. Move containers to a sheltered location protected from temperature fluctuations in winter.

Tips

The low, spreading creeping Jenny will form a dense mat that spills over the edges of your containers and creep into any others you have positioned close by. The contrasting foliage of golden creeping Jenny works well planted with lungwort, blue-leaved hosta or ligularia. Gooseneck loosestrife is a good upright companion plant for a mixed container.

Recommended

L. clethroides (gooseneck loosestrife) is a bushy, upright plant with deep green foliage that turns brilliant bronzy red in fall. Tall spikes, bent like a goose's neck, of white flowers are borne on purple stems in mid- and late summer.

L. nummularia (creeping Jenny) is a prostrate, spreading plant with trailing stems. It bears bright yellow flowers on and off all summer. **'Goldilocks'** (golden creeping Jenny) produces golden foliage with yellow flowers.

L. nummularia with fescue, snapdragon, fan flower and lamium

Not to be confused with purple loosestrife (Lythrum salicaria), which has been banned because of its invasive nature in wetlands, true loosestrife works well just about anywhere in the garden.

Also called: loosestrife **Features:** yellow or white flowers in spring and summer **Height:** 5–90 cm (2–36") **Spread:** 45–90 cm (18–36") **Hardiness:** zones 2–8

Magnolia

Magnolia

M. x 'Betty' (above), *M. stellata* (below)

Magnolias are beautiful, fragrant and versatile, irresistible even to container gardeners who know they will eventually have to move them to the garden.

Growing

Magnolias grow well in **full sun** or **partial shade**. The potting mix should be **humus rich, acidic, moist** and **well drained**. Mix in compost or earthworm castings. Fertilize monthly during the growing season with quarter-strength fertilizer. Magnolias will have to be moved to a garage or shed during winter in most of Canada.

Features: upright to spreading, deciduous small tree or large shrub; white or pink, spring flowers; attractive foliage; smooth, grey bark **Height:** 2.4–5 m (8–15') **Spread:** 1.5–5 m (5–15') **Hardiness:** zones 4–8

Tips

Magnolias are lovely, small trees that make beautiful specimen plants in containers on terraces and patios, as long as they have enough space to spread. Plant tulip bulbs in the planter with your magnolia for an even more impressive spring display.

Recommended

M. x **'Ann'** will form a small, spreading tree with purple-red flowers in late spring.

M. x **'Betty'** will form an upright tree. Dark purple buds open to white flowers in mid-spring.

M. x **'Butterflies'** is an upright tree that bears yellow flowers with red stamens in mid-spring.

M. x *loebneri* (loebner magnolia) forms a rounded to spreading tree. It bears white or pink flowers in mid-spring. **'Merrill'** bears lots of white flowers. It is fast growing and hardy to zone 3.

M. stellata (star magnolia) is a compact, bushy or spreading shrub or small tree. Many-petalled, fragrant, white flowers are borne in early to mid-spring.

Magnolias will eventually grow too large for even a very big planter. They will need to be replaced or root pruned every few years. They can be moved to the garden when they grow too large for their containers.

M. stellata 'Royal Star' (above), *M. stellata* (below)

Maidenhair Fern

Adiantum

A. pedatum with dracaena, oxalis and coleus

These fine-textured plants give mixed containers a light, airy appearance.

These charming and delicate-looking ferns add a graceful touch to any shady container planting. Their unique habit and texture will stand out in any combination.

Growing

Common maidenhair fern grows well in **light to partial shade** but tolerates full shade. The potting mix should be **humus rich, slightly acidic** and **moist**. Fertilize monthly with quarter-strength fertilizer during the growing season. Move northern maidenhair fern to a sheltered location in winter. Bring giant maidenhair fern indoors and keep it in a cool bright room in winter.

Tips

These lovely ferns will do well in any shaded spot. Include them in mixed containers, where they make beautiful, arching companions to other shade-lovers like hosta, lungwort and coral bells. They also look nice with colourful flowers.

Recommended

A. formosum (giant maidenhair fern) is a tender species that is sometimes grown as a houseplant. It has stunning, arching fronds that give the whole plant a cascading appearance. It is worth searching for and including in a mixed container, where it is sure to be an elegant beauty.

A. pedatum (northern maidenhair fern) forms a spreading mound of delicate, arching fronds arranged in a horseshoe or circular pattern. Its light green leaflets stand out against the black stems and turn bright yellow in fall.

Features: deciduous fern; summer and fall foliage; habit **Height:** 30–90 cm (12–36")
Spread: 30–60 cm (12–24")
Hardiness: zones 3–8; tender perennial grown as an annual

Maple
Acer

A. ginnala 'Bailey Compact'

Maples are attractive all year long, boasting delicate flowers in spring, attractive foliage and hanging samaras in summer, vibrant leaf colour in fall and interesting bark and branch structures in winter.

Growing

Maples do well in **full sun** or **light shade**. The potting mix should be **humus rich** and **well drained**. Fertilize no more than monthly with quarter-strength fertilizer during the growing

Maple fruits, called samaras, have wings that act like miniature helicopter rotors and help in seed dispersal.

Features: small, multi-stemmed, deciduous tree or large shrub; colourful or decorative foliage that turns stunning shades of red, yellow and orange in fall **Height:** 60 cm–5 m (2–15') **Spread:** 60 cm–5 m (2–15') **Hardiness:** zones 2–8

A. palmatum 'Bloodgood' (above)

A. japonicum (centre), *A. griseum* (below)

season. Tender maples should be moved into a shed or garage in winter. Hardy maples will do fine in a spot protected from temperature fluctuations.

Tips

Maples can be used as specimen trees in containers on patios or terraces. A Japanese-style garden can be created in containers with a maple or two to add height and volume. Almost all maples can be used to create bonsai specimens.

Recommended

A. ginnala (amur maple) is an extremely hardy, rounded tree with a spreading habit. It has attractive, dark green leaves, bright red samaras and smooth bark with distinctive vertical striping. The fall foliage is often a brilliant crimson. The colour develops best in full sun, but the tree will also grow well in light shade.

A. griseum (paperbark maple) is a rounded to oval tree with exfoliating, orange-brown bark that peels and curls away from the trunk in papery strips. The foliage turns red, orange or yellow in fall. (Zones 4–8)

A. japonicum (fullmoon maple, Japanese maple) is an open, spreading tree or large shrub. The leaves turn stunning shades of yellow, orange or red in fall. (Zones 5–7)

A. palmatum (Japanese maple) is a rounded, spreading or cascading, small tree that develops red, yellow or orange fall colour. Two distinct groups of cultivars have been developed. Types without dissected leaves, derived from *A. p.* var. *atropurpureum,* are grown for their purple foliage. Types with dissected leaves, derived from *A. p.* var. *dissectum,* have foliage so deeply lobed and divided that it appears fern-like or even thread-like. The leaves can be green, red or purple. (Zones 6–8)

Marguerite Daisy

Anthemis

*P*retty, daisy-like flowers almost completely cover the fine, feathery foliage when these plants are in bloom.

Growing

Marguerite daisy grows best in **full sun**. The potting mix should be **well drained**. This plant is drought tolerant. Fertilize monthly with quarter-strength fertlizer. Move hardy plants to a sheltered location in winter. Where they are not hardy, store containers in a shed or garage in winter.

Tips

Marguerite daisies can be planted alone in specimen containers and are also a cheerful addition to mixed containers. The daisy-like flowers have a warm, welcoming appearance that makes them a good choice for containers placed near an entryway.

Recommended

A. marshalliana (marshall chamomile) is a low, mound-forming plant. Its finely divided leaves are covered in long, silvery hairs. Bright golden yellow flowers are borne in summer. (Zones 3–7)

A. punctata subsp. *cupaniana* forms a low mat of silvery grey foliage. It bears yellow-centred, white flowers in early summer. (Zones 6–8)

A. tinctoria (golden marguerite) forms a mounded clump of foliage that is completely covered in bright or pale yellow, daisy-like flowers in summer. '**Grallach Gold**' bears bright golden yellow flowers. '**Moonlight**' bears large, buttery or pale yellow flowers.

A. tinctoria

Shear plants back as flowering finishes to encourage fresh growth and a second flush of flowers.

Also called: golden marguerite **Features:** mounding or spreading perennial; yellow, orange or cream, daisy-like, summer flowers; finely divided or feathery foliage **Height:** 20–90 cm (8–36") **Spread:** 60–90 cm (24–36") **Hardiness:** zones 3–8

Million Bells

Calibrachoa

C. Superbells Series 'Trailing Blue'

Try them with sweet potato vine, asparagus fern and coleus for a riotous display of colour and texture.

Million bells are charming plants that will bloom continuously throughout the growing season.

Growing
Million bells prefer to grow in **full sun**. The potting mix should be **moist** and **well drained**. Fertilize every two weeks during the growing season with half-strength fertilizer. Although they prefer to be watered regularly, million bells are fairly drought resistant in cool and warm climates. Million bells will bloom well into fall.

Tips
Million bells are deservedly popular for planters and hanging baskets. They can stand alone, filling and trailing over the edge of just about any container, and also make lovely additions to mixed containers, where the colourful flowers will stand out against a background in any shade of green, bronze or chartreuse.

Recommended
C. **hybrids** have a dense, trailing habit. They all bear small, yellow-centred flowers that resemble petunias. There are many cultivars available, and more beautiful plants with a wider range of flower colours become available each year. Two main series for these plants are **Million Bells Series** and **Superbells Series**. Both offer plants with flowers in shades of blue, pink, red, yellow, orange or white. Several bicoloured options are also available, including yellow-orange, mottled and pink-veined white.

Also called: calibrachoa **Features:** trailing habit; pink, purple, blue, red, yellow, orange, white or sometimes bicoloured flowers **Height:** 15–30 cm (6–12") **Spread:** up to 60 cm (24") **Hardiness:** tender perennial grown as an annual

Mondo Grass

Ophiopogon

Mondo grass is an excellent accent and contrast plant. The foliage makes a stunning background to highlight any brightly coloured plant or flower.

Growing

Mondo grass grows best in **partial shade** or **light shade**. The potting mix should be **humus rich, moist** and **well drained**. Fertilize monthly during the growing season with quarter- to half-strength fertilizer. Treat these plants like annuals or move containers to an unheated garage or shed in winter to protect them from temperature fluctuations.

Tips

Mondo grass is a low-growing grass that provides a nice, low filler for containers. The foliage contrasts nicely with colourful plants and is eye-catching enough on its own to look attractive when its companions are done blooming.

Recommended

O. japonicus (mondo grass, monkey grass) produces an evergreen mat of lush, dark green, grass-like foliage. Short spikes of white, occasionally lilac-tinged flowers emerge in summer, followed by metallic blue fruit. Many cultivars are available in dwarf forms and variegated forms.

O. planiscapus NIGRA (black mondo grass, black lily turf), a Proven Winners Selection, is a clumping, spreading plant with dark purple, almost black leaves and pink flowers.

O. planiscapus NIGRA

This plant is not a grass at all—it is a member of the lily family.

Features: low, clump-forming grass; uniquely coloured foliage; lavender, pink or white flowers **Height:** 10–30 cm (4–12") **Spread:** 15–30 cm (6–12") **Hardiness:** zones 6–8; grown as an annual

Monkey Flower
Mimulus

M. x hybridus 'Mystic'

A wide range of colours and a floriferous habit make these plants perfect for containers and hanging baskets.

Growing
Monkey flowers prefer **light shade** or **partial shade** with protection from the afternoon sun. The potting mix should be **humus rich** and **moist to wet**. Mix in compost or earthworm castings. Fertilize every two weeks in summer with quarter- to half-strength fertilizer.

Tips
Monkey flowers are excellent in a bog-themed mixed container, as they naturally grow alongside streams. Many of the other moisture-loving plants are foliage plants or flower for only a short time, so these colourful bloomers are a welcome addition.

Recommended
M. aurantiacus is an upright to relaxed plant with glossy, sticky, bright green leaves. It bears dark red, orange or yellow flowers in late summer.

M. x hybridus is a group of upright plants with spotted flowers. 'Calypso' has flowers in a wide range of colours. 'Mystic' is compact, early flowering and offers a wide range of bright flower colours in solids or bicolours.

M. luteus (yellow monkey flower) has a spreading habit and attractive, yellow flowers sometimes spotted with red or purple.

Features: bushy, upright or trailing, semi-hardy perennial; flowers in bright and pastel shades of orange, yellow, burgundy, pink, red, cream or bicolours
Height: 15–30 cm (6–12")
Spread: 30–60 cm (12–24")
Hardiness: zones 6–8; grown as an annual

These plants can be brought indoors at the end of summer and grown as houseplants in a cool, bright room during winter.

Nasturtium

Tropaeolum

T. majus 'Alaska' with ipomoea, impatiens, dracaena and parsley

There is almost nothing as lovely as the exotic red, orange or yellow flowers dotting a planting of nasturtiums as they tumble over the edge of a tall terra-cotta pot.

Growing

Nasturtiums prefer **full sun** but tolerate some shade. The potting mix should be **light, moist** and **well drained**. Too much fertilizer will result in lots of leaves and very few flowers, so fertilize no more than monthly with quarter-strength fertilizer. Let the soil drain completely between waterings.

Tips

Nasturtiums are used in containers and hanging baskets. The climbing varieties can be grown up trellises or left to spill over the edge of a container and ramble around. The bushy selections can be used in mixed containers with other red-, yellow- or orange-flowered plants or with other edible-flowered plants like pansies for a themed container.

Recommended

T. majus is a bushy plant with a trailing or climbing habit. It bears brightly coloured red, yellow or orange flowers all summer. The bright green leaves are round with wavy margins. **'Alaska'** has cream-mottled foliage and a bushy habit. **'Jewel'** has bushy plants with flowers in shades of red, scarlet, pink, yellow, cream or orange, some with darker-veined throats.

The edible leaves and flowers add a peppery flavour to salads.

Features: trailing, climbing or bushy habit; bright red, orange, yellow, burgundy, pink, cream, gold, white or bicoloured flowers; attractive, round, sometimes variegated foliage; edible leaves and flowers **Height:** 30–45 cm (12–18") for dwarf varieties; up to 3 m (10') for trailing varieties **Spread:** equal to height **Hardiness:** annual

Nemesia

Nemesia

N. SUNSATIA PINEAPPLE and others

Nemesias make a bright and colourful addition to the front of a mixed container planting.

Growing

Nemesias grow best in **full sun**. The potting mix should be **slightly acidic, moist** and **well drained**. Regular watering will keep these plants blooming through summer. Fertilize every two weeks with quarter-strength fertilizer when plants are actively growing and blooming.

Tips

Nemesias are beautiful little plants that are best used in mixed containers

---

Features: bushy, mound-forming habit; red, blue, purple, pink, white, yellow, orange or bicoloured flowers **Height:** 15–60 cm (6–24") **Spread:** 10–30 cm (4–12") **Hardiness:** annual; perennial grown as an annual

because they tend to stop blooming during the hottest part of summer.

Recommended

N. **hybrids** are bushy and mound-forming or trailing and have bright green foliage. They bear flowers in shades of blue, purple, white, pink, red or yellow, often in bicolours. **'Bluebird'** bears lavender blue flowers on low, bushy plants. **Carnival Series** plants are compact and bear many flowers in yellow, white, orange, pink or red. **'Compact Innocence'** bears white flowers. **'KLM'** has bicoloured blue and white flowers with yellow throats. **'National Ensign'** ('Red and White') bears bicoloured red and white flowers. SUNSATIA SERIES, a Proven Winners Selection, includes colourful cultivars that may be bushy or trailing and several that are heat resistant.

Nicotiana

Nicotiana

These bushy, sticky plants topped with clusters of tubular flowers attract night-flying pollinators like moths.

Growing

Nicotiana will grow equally well in **full sun, light shade** or **partial shade**. The potting mix should be **humus rich, moist** and **well drained**. Fertilize every two weeks with half-strength fertilizer.

Tips

The dwarf selections seem best suited for small mixed containers, but the taller selections make excellent centre plants with low, bushy and trailing plants surrounding their feet.

Recommended

N. alata is an upright plant that has a strong, sweet fragrance. **Merlin Series** has dwarf plants with red, pink, purple, white or pale green flowers. **Nicki Series** has compact or dwarf plants with fragrant blooms in many colours.

N. **'Lime Green'** is an upright plant that bears clusters of lime green flowers.

N. sylvestris is a tall, upright plant that bears white blooms that are fragrant in the evening.

Nicotiana was originally cultivated for the wonderful scent of its flowers. At first, the flowers were only green and opened only in the evening and at night. In attempts to expand the variety of colours and have the flowers open during the day, the popular scent has, in some cases, been lost.

N. alata Nicki Series and *N. sylvestris* with cleome

Features: sticky, rosette-forming to bushy, upright annual or perennial; red, pink, green, yellow, white or purple, sometimes fragrant flowers **Height:** 30 cm–1.5 m (1–5') **Spread:** 30 cm (12") **Hardiness:** annual; perennial grown as an annual

Oregano

Origanum

O. vulgare var. *hirtum* 'Aureum' with marigold, parsley and tarragon

Oregano is a lovely, fragrant plant with a compact, rounded habit and decorative foliage.

Growing

Oregano grows best in **full sun**. The potting mix should be **neutral to alkaline** and **well drained**. Fertilize no more than once a month with quarter-strength fertilizer. In winter, move hardy plants to a sheltered location; where they are not hardy, move them to an unheated shed or garage.

Tips

Try growing several different oreganos in individual containers of different heights to create a grouping, or plant different herbs in each pot for a more varied display.

Recommended

O. laevigatum is a shrubby, upright perennial that bears rosy purple flowers.

O. vulgare var. *hirtum* (oregano, Greek oregano) is a low-growing, bushy plant with hairy, grey-green leaves and white flowers. **'Aureum'** has bright golden leaves and pink flowers. **'Aureum Crispum'** has a spreading habit and curly, golden leaves. **'Zorba Red'** has a spreading habit with bright, red-purple bracts and white flowers. **'Zorba White'** has greenish bracts and white flowers.

In Greek, oros means "mountain" and ganos means "joy" or "beauty," so oregano translates as "joy" or "beauty of the mountain."

Features: bushy perennial; fragrant, sometimes colourful foliage; white or pink, summer flowers
Height: 25–60 cm (10–24")
Spread: 20–30 cm (8–12")
Hardiness: zones 5–8

Osteospermum

Osteospermum

Osteospermum's daisy-like flowers, with their unique colours, really stand out in a mixed container.

Growing

Osteospermum grows best in **full sun**. The potting mix should be **light, moist** and **well drained**. Fertilize every two weeks with half-strength fertilizer. Deadhead to encourage new growth and more flowers. Young plants can be pinched to encourage bushiness.

Tips

Osteospermum's daisy-like flowers mix well with other annuals like petunia and verbena, or mix them with other daisy-like flowers for a daisy-themed container. Osteospermum blooms best during cool weather and will brighten up your containers in fall when other plants start to fade.

Recommended

O. ecklonis can grow upright to almost prostrate. The species is almost never grown in favour of its cultivars. **Passion mix** includes heat-tolerant plants with pink, rose, purple or white flowers with deep blue centres and was an All-America Selections winner in 1999. **Starwhirls Series** has unique, spoon-shaped petals. **'Starwhirls Antaris'** bears deep pink flowers. The petals of **'Starwhirls Vega'** are white on the upper surface and pink beneath.

O. **Symphony Series** has mound-forming, heat-tolerant plants that flower well throughout summer. **'Lemon'** bears yellow flowers. **'Orange'** bears tangerine orange flowers. **'Peach'** bears peachy pink flowers. **'Vanilla'** bears white flowers.

O. SOPRANO LIGHT PURPLE from the Proven Winners Selection SOPRANO SERIES

You may find African daisy listed as either Dimorphotheca *or* Osteospermum. Dimorphotheca *is a closely related genus that formerly included all the plants now listed as* Osteospermum.

Also called: African daisy, cape daisy
Features: white, peach, orange, yellow, pink, lavender or purple flowers, often with darker centres **Height:** 30–50 cm (12–20")
Spread: 25–50 cm (10–20") **Hardiness:** perennial or subshrub grown as an annual

Oxalis

Oxalis

O. vulcanicola 'Zinfandel' and others

Tiny, decorative pots of O. crassipes *are often found in garden centres and gift shops around St. Patrick's Day.*

Features: bushy or spreading habit; colourful foliage; yellow, white or pink flowers
Height: 15–30 cm (6–12")
Spread: 15–30 cm (6–12") or more
Hardiness: tender perennial grown as an annual

Oxalis readily fills little spaces with dense, lustrous foliage and teeny, tiny flowers that never cease to amaze.

Growing

Oxalis prefers **full sun** or **partial shade** and tolerates full shade with reduced flowering. The potting mix should be **humus rich** and **well drained**. Fertilize every two weeks with quarter-strength fertilizer.

Tips

Oxalis is becoming increasingly popular in container culture, with new varieties appearing annually. Tightly packed, fine foliage and prolific flowering are qualities ideal for containers of all sizes and styles. Oxalis works well mixed with other plants and is equally stunning all alone in a hanging basket.

Recommended

O. crassipes is a vigorous species with bright green leaves and lemon yellow flowers. The cultivars are more often available than the species. **'Alba'** is a mound-forming cultivar with green leaves and tiny, white flowers. It is tolerant of extreme heat and drought. **'Rosea'** has pink flowers.

O. renellii is a vigorous, shade-loving species. It produces large, shamrock-shaped foliage and dainty flowers. Cultivars to watch for are selections from the CHARMED SERIES.

O. vulcanicola is a small, bushy, spreading plant with reddish stems, green foliage flushed with red, and yellow flowers with purple-red veining. **'Copper Tones'** and **'Molten Lava'** have gold foliage with a touch of rust and buttery yellow flowers at the tips of reddish stems. **'Zinfandel'** produces dark burgundy, almost black foliage and tiny, vivid yellow blooms.

Pansy
Viola

V. x wittrockiana cultivar with vinca, coral bells and dracaena

Colourful and cheerful, pansy flowers are a welcome sight in spring after a long, dreary winter.

Growing

Pansies prefer **full sun** but tolerate partial shade. The potting mix should be **moist** and **well drained**. Fertilize every two weeks during the growing season with quarter-strength fertilizer. Pansies do best when the weather is cool and often die back completely in summer.

Johnny-jump-ups self-seed prolifically and may turn up from year to year in not only the container they were growing in, but other containers too.

Features: blue, purple, red, orange, yellow, pink or white, bicoloured or multi-coloured flowers **Height:** 8–25 cm (3–10") **Spread:** 15–30 cm (6–12") **Hardiness:** zones 5–8

V. x *wittrockiana* cultivar with calla lily (above)
V. x *wittrockiana* (below)

Plants may rejuvenate in fall, but it is often easier to plant new ones.

Tips

Pansies make good companions for spring-flowering bulbs and primroses. A pot of spring pansies set where you can see it from indoors will remind you that summer is just around the corner.

Recommended

V. cornuta (horned violet, viola) is a low-growing, spreading plant. The flowers are usually in shades of blue, purple or white. **Chalon hybrids** bear ruffled, bicoloured or multi-coloured flowers in shades of blue, red, rose or white. **Sorbet Series** has a wide colour range. Planted in fall, they flower until the ground freezes and may surprise you with another show in spring. **'Sorbet Yesterday, Today and Tomorrow'** bears flowers that open white and gradually turn purple as they mature.

V. tricolor (Johnny-jump-up) is a popular species. The flowers are purple, white and yellow, usually in combination, although several varieties have flowers in a single colour, often purple.

V. x wittrockiana (pansy) comes in blue, purple, red, orange, yellow, pink or white, often multi-coloured or with face-like markings. **Antique Shades mix** offers pastel combinations of plum, yellow, apricot, rust and cream. **Can Can mix** bears frilly flowers with ruffled edges in bicoloured and multi-coloured combinations of yellow, purple, red, white, pink and blue. **Imperial Series** includes plants that bear large flowers in a range of unique colours. **'Imperial Frosty Rose'** has flowers with deep rose pink centres that gradually pale to white near the edges of the petals.

Parsley

Petroselinum

P. crispum with others

The tightly curled leaves and bright green colour of parsley provide an unmatched display to fill in the spaces among the other plants in your containers.

Growing

Parsley grows well in **full sun** or **partial shade**. The potting mix should be **humus rich, moist** and **well drained**. Fertilize every two weeks with quarter-strength fertilizer during the growing season. Direct sow seeds because the plants resent transplanting.

Tips

Containers of parsley can be kept close to the house for easy picking if you are growing it for eating or garnish—you could have several pots containing different herbs. Parsley is also a fantastic mixer plant for containers. Its bushy growth fills in quickly, and the bright green creates a good background for bright red, scarlet or orange flowers in particular.

Recommended

P. crispum forms a clump of bright green, divided leaves. This plant is biennial but is usually grown as an annual because it is the leaves that are desired, not the flowers or seeds. Cultivars may have flat or curly leaves. Flat leaves are more flavourful and curly are more decorative. Dwarf cultivars are also available.

Parsley leaves make a tasty and nutritious addition to salads. Tear freshly picked leaves and sprinkle them over or mix them into your mixed greens.

Features: clump-forming biennial; attractive foliage **Height:** 20–60 cm (8–24")
Spread: 30–60 cm (12–24")
Hardiness: zones 5–8; grown as an annual

Penstemon

Penstemon

P. LILLIPUT ROSE, a Proven Winners Selection, with nemesia and coleus

Mix one or two penstemons into your containers, and they will be sure to attract hummingbirds to your garden.

Growing

Penstemons prefer **full sun** but tolerate partial shade. The potting mix should be **well drained**. These plants are quite drought tolerant. Fertilize every two weeks with half-strength fertilizer. Move containers to a sheltered location protected from temperature fluctuations in winter.

Tips

These plants tend to be tall and slender and are prone to falling over unless they are surrounded by supportive neighbours. They are ideal for mixed containers.

Also called: beard-tongue **Features:** white, yellow, pink, purple or red, spring, summer or fall flowers **Height:** 45 cm–1.5 m (18"–5') **Spread:** 30–60 cm (12–24") **Hardiness:** zones 3–8

Recommended

P. barbatus (beardlip penstemon) is an upright, rounded perennial. Red or pink flowers are borne from early summer to early fall. **'Hyacinth Mix'** is a mix of pink, lilac, blue and scarlet. **'Prairie Dusk'** has tall spikes of tubular, pink-purple flowers. **'White Bedder'** bears white flowers that are tinged with pink.

P. digitalis (foxglove penstemon) is a very hardy, upright, semi-evergreen perennial. It bears white flowers, often veined with purple, all summer. **'Husker Red'** has red stems and red-purple new foliage. The flowers are white and veined with red. (Zones 4–8)

P. fruticosus **'Purple Haze'** is a mound-forming subshrub with evergreen foliage. It bears prolific, purple flowers in late spring. When placed near a wall edge or overhang, it will trail over the edge, creating a showy display. (Zones 4–8)

Perilla

Perilla

*P*erilla has been used for centuries as a medicinal plant in Chinese medicine and as an Asian culinary herb. Recently, breeders have introduced more decorative selections to the market, making perilla a highly sought-after plant.

Growing

Perilla prefers **full sun** or **partial shade**. The potting mix should be **fertile, moist** and **well drained**. Soil amended with compost or well-composted manure is of added benefit.

Tips

Perilla is the perfect alternative to coleus and is an ideal complement to brightly coloured annuals and perennials in decorative containers.

Recommended

P. frutescens is a vigorous annual with deeply toothed, medium green, purple-flecked, cinnamon-lemon–flavoured leaves. Tiny, white flowers are borne on spikes in summer, but this annual is grown more for its ornate, colourful foliage. **'Magilla'** ('Magilla Purple') bears multi-coloured leaves of purple, green, white and pink, and **'Magilla Vanilla'** bears white and green leaves.

P. 'Magellanica,' a Proven Selections plant from Proven Winners, and others

Perilla is well known for its tolerance of summer heat and will easily compete with some of the most aggressive summer annuals available.

Also called: magilla perilla
Features: bushy, vigorous annual; ornate, colourful foliage **Height:** 30–60 cm (12–24")
Spread: 30–60 cm (12–24")
Hardiness: annual

Persicaria

Persicaria

P. affinis 'Dimity'

Persicaria flowers can be dried and used in arrangements.

Also called: fleece flower, knotweed
Features: mat- or clump-forming perennial;
red, pink or white, summer flowers; decorative foliage **Height:** 15–60 cm (6–24")
Spread: 30–90 cm (12–36")
Hardiness: zones 3–8

Small and sturdy, persicaria provides a bright, summer-long display of little flower spikes.

Growing

Persicarias grow best in **full sun** or **partial shade**. The potting mix should be **moist** and **well drained**. Fertilize no more than monthly with quarter-strength fertilizer. Move containers to a sheltered location protected from temperature fluctuations in winter.

Tips

Himalayan knotweed has a natural appearance that lends itself well to wildflower-themed mixed containers. Its low habit and compact growth also make it useful as a filler plant for containers where taller plants dominate. Red dragon knotweed has showy foliage that contrasts well with other plants and flowers.

Recommended

P. affinis '**Dimity**' (Himalayan knotweed) is a mat-forming, evergreen perennial that grows 15–20 cm (6–8") tall and 30–60 cm (12–24") wide. The leathery foliage turns a bronzy red colour in fall. Short spikes of red flowers are held above the foliage and fade to pink with age.

P. microcephala '**Red Dragon**' (red dragon knotweed) is a vigorous, clump-forming perennial. It produces red stems with metallic, deep burgundy leaves marked with a plum- or mint-coloured chevron. The foliage becomes greener later in the season, accented by a red leaf margin and a red chevron. White, insignificant flowers emerge in summer. This cultivar grows 60 cm (24") tall and 75–90 cm (30–36") wide. (Zones 5–8)

Petunia

Petunia

*F*or speedy growth, prolific blooming, ease of care and a huge number of varieties, petunias are hard to
beat.

Growing

Petunias prefer **full sun**. The potting
mix should be **well drained**. Fertilize no
more than monthly during the growing
season with quarter-strength fertilizer.
Pinch halfway back in mid-summer to
keep plants bushy and to encourage new
growth and flowers.

Tips

Use petunias in containers and hanging
baskets. Planted alone, their bushy
growth will fill a container and spill
over the edges. The rich colours of their
flowers also make them excellent companions for other annuals as well as for
any container plantings of shrubs or
small trees.

Recommended

P. x *hybrida* is a large group of popular,
sun-loving annuals that fall into three
categories: the grandifloras, with the
largest flowers; the multifloras, bearing
many medium-sized flowers; and the
millifloras, with the smallest flowers.
There are countless varieties of petunias
available within these categories, with
new ones introduced each year. The
Supertunia Series predominantly offers
flowers in a wide range of pinks and
purples, but there are also red, white
and yellow selections as well as double
flowers.

*The rekindling of interest in petunias
resulted largely from the development of
many exciting new varieties.*

P. x *hybrida* with english ivy and reed palm

Features: bushy to trailing habit; summer
flowers in shades of pink, blue, purple, red,
coral, yellow, white or bicolours
Height: 15–45 cm (6–18")
Spread: 30–60 cm (12–24") or wider
Hardiness: annual

Phormium

Phormium

P. tenax cultivar with echivaria and hens and chicks

These bold and impressive plants create quite an impact. They are bound to become the focal point of any planting.

Growing

Phormiums grow best in **full sun** but appreciate some protection from the hot afternoon sun. The potting mix should be **moist** and **well drained**. Fertilize every two weeks during the growing season with half-strength fertilizer. Plants grown in containers can be over-wintered in a bright, cool, frost-free location indoors.

Tips

Use phormiums in container plantings near entryways and walkways. Their bold and exotic foliage will draw the eye and encourage visitors to come closer for a better look.

Recommended

P. 'Sundowner' forms a clump of broad, upright foliage. The light, bronzy green foliage is margined with pink and yellow.

P. tenax (New Zealand flax) forms a large clump of long, stiff, dark green leaves with grey-green undersides. 'Aurora' has bronzy green leaves striped with pink, yellow and red. 'Veitchia-num' has cream-striped, green leaves.

P. 'Yellow Wave' forms a clump of yellow-green leaves striped with darker green.

Also called: New Zealand flax
Features: clump-forming habit; green, black, red or yellow, often multi-coloured and striped foliage **Height:** 60 cm–2.4 m (2–8')
Spread: 60 cm–2.4 m (2–8')
Hardiness: zone 8; tender perennial grown as an annual

Large, loose spikes of small flowers are sometimes produced in summer.

Piggyback Plant

Tolmiea

Piggyback plant uniquely produces new plantlets from the surface of an existing leaf, hence the common name.

Growing

Piggyback plant grows best in **full shade, light shade** or **partial shade** with protection from the hot afternoon sun. The potting mix should be **moist** and **well drained**. Fertilize monthly during the growing season with quarter-strength fertilizer. Keep plants in a cool, bright room in winter where they are not hardy. Where they are hardy, move plants to a sheltered location protected from temperature fluctuations.

Tips

Piggyback plant is often grown in hanging baskets. The mounded leaves are weighted down by newly produced foliage, creating a cascading appearance. It can also be grown in containers where you can observe the intriguing foliage from above. This plant is an ideal addition to an understorey-themed container or for a container on a heavily shaded balcony.

Recommended

T. menziesii is a clump-forming plant with hairy, heart-shaped leaves with toothed edges. Small plantlets emerge where the leaf and stem join. Tiny, tubular, greenish, insignificant flowers open along one side of the leaf. **'Variegata'** has yellow-splashed leaves, and **'Taff's Gold'** produces both solid and variegated leaves.

T. menziesii

Tolmiea was named after Dr. William Fraser Tolmie (1812–1886). He was a surgeon at the Hudson's Bay Company depot at Fort Vancouver.

Also called: thousand mothers, youth-on-age
Features: clump-forming perennial; decorative, piggyback foliage **Height:** 30–45 cm (12–18") **Spread:** 30–45 cm (12–18")
Hardiness: zones 6–8; grown as an annual

Plectranthus
Plectranthus

P. 'Vanilla Twist,' a Proven Winners Selection, with sedge, fountain grass, english ivy and coleus

These mound-forming plants, with their often-aromatic foliage, eventually develop a more trailing habit.

Growing
Plectranthus grows best in **light shade** or **partial shade**. The potting mix should be **moist** and **well drained**. Fertilize every two weeks during the growing season with quarter- to half-strength fertilizer.

Tips
These trailing plants make fabulous fillers for hanging baskets and mixed containers. Place them near a walkway or other area where people will be able to brush past the plants and smell the spicy-scented foliage.

Recommended
P. argentatus is an upright to spreading plant with silvery green, hairy stems and leaves. It bears clusters of small, bluish white flowers near the ends of stems in summer.

P. forsteri is a mounding, then trailing, plant with light green, slightly hairy leaves and clusters of small, white or pale purple flowers in summer. '**Marginatus**' has cream-edged leaves.

P. madagascariensis (mintleaf) is a creeping, spreading plant with fleshy leaves that smell of mint when crushed. '**Variegated Mintleaf**' has cream and green variegated leaves.

The trailing stems root easily from cuttings; start some in late summer to grow indoors through winter.

Also called: Mexican mint **Features:** bushy to trailing habit; decorative foliage **Height:** 20–30 cm (8–12") **Spread:** about 90 cm (36") **Hardiness:** annual; tender perennial grown as an annual

Rose

Rosa

R. 'Knock Out' (above & below)

There are many roses that will thrive in containers, though most will eventually have to be moved to the garden.

Growing

Roses grow best in **full sun**. The potting mix should be **humus rich, slightly acidic, moist** and **well drained**. Fertilize every two weeks with half-strength fertilizer. Deadhead lightly to keep plants tidy and to encourage prolific blooming, except Hansa and Knock Out, which develop attractive hips after the flowers are done.

Features: rounded to arching shrub; often fragrant, mid-summer to fall flowers; disease resistant **Height:** 30 cm–1.2 m (1–4') **Spread:** 30 cm–1.2 m (1–4') **Hardiness:** zones 3–8

R. 'Hansa' (above), R. 'Cupcake' (below)

Tips

Bushy modern shrub roses, miniature roses and hardy roses like the rugosas are the best choices for containers. The miniatures make good companions for mixed containers, while the larger, shrubbier roses make good focal pieces, perhaps with white-flowered, trailing plants like bacopas planted around them.

Recommended

R. **'Cupcake'** is a compact, bushy miniature shrub rose with glossy, green foliage. It produces clusters of light to medium pink flowers all summer. It grows 30–45 cm (12–18") tall, with an equal spread. (Zones 5–8)

R. **'George Vancouver'** is a hardy, mound-forming Explorer rose that maintains a neat, rounded habit. The medium red, double flowers may be borne singly or in clusters of up to six. It grows about 60 cm (24") tall and wide.

R. **'Hansa'** is a hardy, arching rugosa rose with deeply veined, glossy, leathery foliage. The fragrant, mauve purple to mauve red, double flowers are followed by scarlet hips. It grows about 1.2 m (4') tall and wide.

R. **'Knock Out'** has an attractive, rounded form with glossy, green leaves that turn to shades of burgundy in fall. The bright, cherry red flowers are borne in clusters almost all summer and fall. Orange-red hips last well into winter. It grows about 1.2 m (4') tall and wide. (Zones 4–8)

Miniature roses like Cupcake can be overwintered indoors in a cool, bright room.

Rosemary

Rosmarinus

These pretty little ever-greens have fragrant foliage and varied habits that make them worth growing whether you have an herb collection or not.

Growing

Rosemary prefers **full sun** but tolerates partial shade if it is overwintered indoors. The potting mix should be evenly **moist** and **well drained**; this plant doesn't like wet soil, but doesn't like to dry out completely either. Fertilize no more than once a month during the growing season with quarter-strength fertilizer. This tender shrub must be moved indoors in winter and kept in the brightest location available.

Tips

Rosemary can be grown in a container as a specimen or with other plants. Low-growing, spreading plants can be grown in hanging baskets.

Recommended

R. officinalis is a dense, bushy, evergreen shrub with narrow, dark green leaves. The habit varies somewhat among cultivars from strongly upright to prostrate and spreading. Flowers are usually in shades of blue, but pink-flowered cultivars are available.

R. officinalis 'Prostratus'

To keep plants bushy, pinch the tips back. The bits you pinch off can be used to flavour roast chicken, soups and stews.

Features: evergreen shrub; attractive, fragrant foliage; bright blue, sometimes pink, summer flowers
Height: 20 cm–1.2 m (8"–4')
Spread: 30 cm–1.2 m (1–4')
Hardiness: zone 8; overwintered indoors

Rush

Juncus

J. effusus 'Spiralis' with impatiens

Rushes are popular, eye-catching plants, particularly the curly- or spiral-leaved cultivars, which prove fascinating to gardeners and visitors alike.

Growing

Rushes grow well in **full sun** or **partial shade**. The potting mix should be **acidic** and **moist to wet**. Fertilize no more than monthly with a quarter-strength fertilizer. Move containers to a sheltered location protected from temperature fluctuations where plants are hardy. Grow them as annuals where they aren't hardy.

Tips

Plant rushes in moist containers with other water-loving plants like monkey

flower, iris and sedge. They can even be grown in shallow, gravel-filled water dishes, where they can be used to create a unique, living centrepiece for your patio table.

Recommended

J. effusus (soft rush) forms a tufted clump of long, flexible, stem-like leaves and bears insignificant flowers in summer. The species is rarely grown. **'Spiralis'** (corkscrew rush), a Proven Winners Selection, forms a tangled-looking mass of curling and corkscrew-like leaves, and cultivars with more corkscrew-like leaves are becoming available. **'Variegated Spiral Rush'** has white-streaked leaves. (Zones 6–8)

J. inflexus (hard rush) forms a clump of stiff, stem-like leaves. **'Afro'** has more tightly spiraled stems than *J. effusus* 'Spiralis.'

Features: marginally aquatic perennial; decorative, stem-like leaves **Height:** 45–60 cm (18–24") **Spread:** 30 cm (12") **Hardiness:** zones 4–8

Salvia

Salvia

Proven Winners Selection *S. officinalis* 'Purpurescens' with osteospermum, sedge and others

Spikes of pretty, little flowers and attractive mounds of foliage help these plants blend into mixed containers.

Growing

Salvias grow best in **full sun** but tolerate light shade. The potting mix should be **humus rich, moist** and **well drained**. Fertilize every two weeks during the growing season with quarter- to half-strength fertilizer. Move containers to a sheltered location protected from

Sage has been used since at least ancient Greek times as a medicinal and culinary herb and continues to be widely used for both those purposes today.

Also called: sage **Features:** bushy perennial or annual; decorative, sometimes fragrant foliage; red, blue, purple, burgundy, pink, orange, salmon, yellow, cream, white or bicoloured, summer flowers **Height:** 30–60 cm (12–24") **Spread:** 20–60 cm (8–24") **Hardiness:** zones 4–8; tender perennial grown as an annual

S. splendens 'Sizzler White' with basil (above)
S. officinalis 'Icterina' (below)

temperature fluctuations in winter. Some are annuals or are treated like annuals where they won't survive winter.

Tips

Salvias are attractive plants that combine well with a wide variety of other plants and with each other. Use common sage with other edible herbs like rosemary, basil and thyme for a fragrant, edible container. The bright blue flowers of blue sage contrast with orange or yellow flowers.

Recommended

S. farinacea (blue sage, mealy cup sage) has bright blue flowers clustered along stems powdered with silver. 'Victoria' is a popular cultivar with silvery foliage and deep blue flowers. (Zone 8)

S. greggii (autumn sage) is a compact, shrubby perennial. It bears red, pink, purple or yellow flowers. 'Raspberry Royale' bears raspberry red flowers. (Zones 7–8)

S. officinalis is a woody, mounding plant with soft, grey-green leaves. It bears light purple flowers in early and mid-summer. Many cultivars with attractive foliage are available, including the silver-leaved 'Berggarten,' the purple-leaved 'Purpurea,' the yellow-margined 'Icterina' and the purple-green and cream variegated 'Tricolor,' which has a pink flush to the new growth.

S. splendens (salvia, scarlet sage) is a bushy perennial grown as an annual. It bears bright red flowers. Recently, cultivars have become available in white, pink, purple or orange. 'Salsa' bears solid and bicoloured flowers in shades of red, orange, purple, burgundy, cream or pink. **Sizzler Series** bears flowers in burgundy, lavender, pink, plum, red, salmon, or white and salmon bicoloured.

Scarlet Runner Bean

Phaseolus

Beautiful plants that also provide tasty vegetables are always a welcome addition to the container garden.

Growing

Scarlet runner beans grow best in **full sun**. The potting mix should be **moist** and **well drained**. Fertilize monthly with quarter- to half-strength fertilizer. These beans should be placed near something they can twine around. A porch railing or obelisk is suitable.

Tips

Scarlet runner beans have a carefree habit, twisting and twining around each other and any structure you can provide for them. They are delightful when grown in a container with an obelisk-type frame to climb up. Create a similar look simply by poking three or four long poles into the container and tying them together at the top. Plant these beans in a hanging basket for a unique display.

Recommended

P. coccineus is a twining, annual vine. Scarlet red flowers are borne in clusters in summer, followed by long, edible pods. **Var. *alba*** (Dutch runner bean) bears white flowers. **'Painted Lady'** bears red and white bicoloured flowers.

P. coccineus

The edible, dark green pods are tender when young and are best eaten before they become stringy and tough.

Features: twining vine; red, white or bicoloured, summer flowers; edible fruit **Height:** 1.8–2.4 m (6–8') **Spread:** 30 cm–1.8 m (1–6') **Hardiness:** annual

Sedge
Carex

C. buchananii, from Proven Winners,
with argyranthemum and others

*Sedges are native to moist wetlands. In
the wild, their dense, tufted clumps can
mislead hikers into believing the ground is
more solid than it is.*

Features: tuft-forming perennial; interesting,
colourful foliage; attractive habit
Height: 30 cm–1.2 m (1–4')
Spread: 30 cm–1.2 m (1–4')
Hardiness: zones 5–8

With its green, blue, rust, bronze
or gold foliage, sedge allows the
gardener to add broad, colourful strokes
or bright accents to the landscape.

Growing

Sedges grow well in **full sun to partial
shade**. The potting mix should be **neutral to slightly alkaline** and **moist to
wet**. 'Frosted Curls' is more drought tolerant. Fertilize every two weeks during
the growing season with quarter-strength fertilizer. Move containers to
an unheated shed or garage where they

will be protected from temperature fluctuations in winter, or grow them as annuals where they aren't hardy.

Tips

Sedges offer colourful foliage and rustic texture to contrast with other moisture-loving plants. The cascading habit of many of these grass-like plants makes them an interesting choice to grow as specimens in containers. Space them evenly around your patio or terrace for a formal display. The fine foliage of 'Frosted Curls' contrasts well with coarse-textured plants.

Recommended

C. buchananii (leatherleaf sedge) forms a dense clump or tuft of narrow, arching, orange-brown leaves. (Zones 6–8)

C. comans 'Frosted Curls' (New Zealand hair sedge) is a compact, clump-forming, evergreen perennial with fine-textured, pale green, weeping foliage. The foliage appears almost iridescent, with unusual curled and twisted tips. (Zones 7–8)

C. elata 'Aurea' (Bowles' golden sedge) forms a clump of arching, grass-like, yellow leaves with green edges. It bears spikes of tiny, brown or green flowers in early summer.

C. morrowii 'Aureovariegata' (variegated Japanese sedge) forms low tufts of drooping, green-and-yellow-striped foliage. (Zones 6–8)

C. pendula (drooping sedge, weeping sedge) forms a clump of graceful, arching, grass-like, green leaves. Drooping spikes of brown flowers are borne on long stems in late spring and early summer.

C. flagellifera TOFFEE TWIST a Proven Winners Selection, with sedge, petunia, sweet flag and argyranthemum (above)
C. comans 'Frosted Curls' (below)

Sedum

Sedum

Sedum with lavender

Early-summer pruning of upright species and hybrids encourages compact, bushy growth but can delay flowering.

Many sedums are grown for their foliage, which can range in colour from steel grey-blue and green to red and burgundy. The flowers are an added bonus.

Growing
Sedums prefer **full sun** but tolerate partial shade. The potting mix should be **neutral to alkaline** and very **well drained**. Fertilize no more than once a month during the growing season with half-strength fertilizer. Move containers to a sheltered location protected from temperature fluctuations in winter.

Tips
Low-growing sedums make wonderful filler plants for mixed containers, where many of them will grow over the edge of the pot. They can also be grown in low, wide dishes to be placed on a stairway so that they cascade over the edge of the dish and down the stairs. Taller selections make good contrast plants for mixed containers.

Recommended
S. acre (gold moss stonecrop) is a low-growing, wide-spreading plant that bears small, yellow-green flowers.

S. 'Autumn Joy' (autumn joy sedum) is a popular upright hybrid. The flowers open pink or red and later fade to deep bronze.

S. spectabile (showy stonecrop) is an upright species with pink flowers. Cultivars are available.

S. spurium (two-row stonecrop) forms a low, wide mat of foliage with deep pink or white flowers. Many cultivars are available and are often grown for their colourful foliage.

Also called: stonecrop **Features:** mat-forming or upright perennial; yellow, white, red or pink, summer to fall flowers; decorative, fleshy foliage **Height:** 5–60 cm (2–24") **Spread:** 30–60 cm (12–24") **Hardiness:** zones 3–8

Serviceberry

Amelanchier

The *Amelanchier* species are first-rate North American natives, bearing lacy, white flowers in spring, followed by edible berries. In fall the foliage colour ranges from glowing apricot to deep red.

Growing

Serviceberries grow well in **full sun** or **light shade**. The potting mix should be **acidic, humus rich, moist** and **well drained**. Fertilize every two weeks during the growing season with quarter-strength fertilizer. Move containers to a sheltered location protected from temperature fluctuations in winter.

Tips

With spring flowers, edible fruit, attractive leaves that turn red in fall and often artistic branch growth, serviceberries make beautiful specimen plants or even small shade trees for large containers.

Recommended

A. arborea (downy serviceberry, juneberry) is a small, single- or multi-stemmed tree that produces clusters of white flowers in spring, followed by berries that ripen to dark purple in summer. The foliage turns yellow, orange and red in fall. (Zones 4–8)

A. canadensis (shadblow serviceberry) is a large, upright, suckering shrub. White, spring flowers are followed by edible, purple summer fruit. The leaves turn orange, scarlet and red in fall.

A. stolonifera (running serviceberry) is a small, suckering shrub. It bears white spring flowers and purple summer fruit, and the leaves turn bright shades of yellow, orange and red in fall. (Zones 4–8)

A. canadensis

Serviceberry fruit can be used in place of blueberries in any recipe, having a similar but generally sweeter flavour.

Also called: saskatoon, juneberry, billberry
Features: single- or multi-stemmed, deciduous large shrub or small tree; spring or early-summer flowers; edible fruit; fall colour; habit; bark **Height:** 1.2–4.5 m (4–15')
Spread: 1.2–4.5 m (4–15')
Hardiness: zones 3–8

Snapdragon

Antirrhinum

A. *majus* cultivar

Snapdragons are interesting and long lasting in fresh flower arrangements. The buds continue to mature and open long after the spike has been cut.

Features: clump-forming habit; white, cream, yellow, orange, red, maroon, pink, purple or bicoloured; summer flowers; glossy, green through bronze foliage
Height: 15 cm–1.2 m (6"–4')
Spread: 15–30 cm (6–12") **Hardiness:** tender perennial grown as an annual

ardeners of all ages love the magic of these flowers, which look like delightful, tiny dragon heads.

Growing

Snapdragons prefer **full sun** but tolerate light shade or partial shade. The potting mix should be **humus rich, neutral to alkaline** and **well drained**. Fertilize every two weeks during the growing season with quarter- to half-strength fertilizer. To encourage bushier growth, pinch the tips of the plants while they are young. Cut off the flower spikes as they fade to promote further blooming.

Tips

Snapdragons are bushy plants of variable height that look lovely planted alone or in mixed containers. There is even a trailing variety that does well in hanging baskets. The strong, upright, vividly coloured flower spikes contrast beautifully with arching grasses and broad, leafy plants like hosta.

Recommended

A. majus is a bushy, clump-forming plant from which flower spikes emerge in summer. Many cultivars are available. Dwarf varieties grow up to 30 cm (12") tall. **'Floral Showers'** grows 15–20 cm (6–8") tall. This plant bears flowers in a wide range of solid colours and bicolours. **'Lampion'** has a trailing habit and cascades up to 90 cm (36"), making it a great plant for hanging baskets. Medium-height snapdragons grow 30–60 cm (12–24") tall. **'Black Prince'** bears striking, dark purple-red flowers set against bronzy green foliage. Giant cultivars can grow 90 cm–1.2 m (3–4') tall. **Rocket Series** cultivars produce long spikes of brightly coloured flowers in many shades and have good heat tolerance.

A. majus cultivar (above & below)

The genus Antirrhinum, *from the Greek, is translated as* anti, *"against," and* rhis, *"snout," based on the appearance of the flower.*

Snow-in-Summer

Cerastium

C. tomentosum

Snow-in-summer is a tough-as-nails plant that thrives even when neglected.

Growing

Snow-in-summer grows best in **full sun** or **partial shade,** with protection from the hot afternoon sun. The potting mix should be **well drained**. Fertilize no more than monthly during the growing season with quarter-strength fertilizer. Trim plants back after flowering is complete to encourage new growth and to keep plants looking tidy. Move containers to a sheltered location protected from temperature fluctuations in winter.

Tips

Many gardeners have shied away from this potentially invasive plant, but it is this very quality that makes it a great container plant. It can only spread as far as the pot allows, and it is hardy and attractive. When using it in a mixed container, be sure to use it with other vigorous plants. It makes a good choice for planting beneath a shrub or tree in a large container.

Recommended

C. tomentosum forms a low mat of silvery grey foliage and bears white flowers in late spring.

This Mediterranean native looks lovely spilling over the edge of a decorative terracotta container.

Features: low, spreading perennial; silvery foliage; white, late-spring flowers; very hardy
Height: 5–30 cm (2–12")
Spread: 90 cm (36") or more
Hardiness: zones 1–8

Spider Plant

Chlorophytum

The grass-like, narrow leaf blades arch gracefully as they grow, creating a spider-like effect, and the long, trailing stems cascade over the pot's edge and carry small plantlets that resemble baby spiders dangling from a silky thread.

Growing

Spider plants grow best in **light shade** or **partial shade** with protection from the hot afternoon sun. The potting mix should be **moist** and **well drained**. Plants are fairly drought tolerant. Fertilize every two weeks with quarter-strength fertilizer. Plants can be moved indoors in winter, but it is often easier to snip off a few of the baby plantlets and grow those over winter to use the following spring.

Tips

Spider plants make good filler plants for mixed containers. They grow quickly and produce flowers and stems of little plantlets while still quite young. The green or variegated leaves will brighten up a container shared with darker-leaved plants like coral bells and begonias.

Recommended

C. comosum forms a clump of graceful, arching, grass-like leaves. Flowering stems emerge from the rosette bearing tiny, white flowers and young plantlets. The stems are pendant, weighed down by the plantlets. **'Milky Way'** has creamy leaf margins. **'Variegatum'** has cream to white leaf margins. **'Vittatum'** has leaves with a white central stripe and green margins.

C. comosum and C. comosum 'Vittatum'

Spider plants are incredibly adaptable, tolerating a wide range of conditions including heat or cold, sun or shade and humid or dry air.

Features: clump-forming habit; decorative, arching, strap-like foliage; stems of trailing or dangling plantlets **Height:** 30 cm (12") **Spread:** 60–90 cm (24–36") **Hardiness:** tender perennial grown as an annual or overwintered indoors

Spruce
Picea

P. glauca var. albertiana 'Conica'

Spruces frequently produce branch mutations, and it is often from these that the dwarf selections are developed.

Features: conical or columnar, evergreen tree or shrub; attractive foliage; varied habit **Height:** 60 cm–1.8 m (2–6') **Spread:** 60 cm–1.2 m (2–4') **Hardiness:** zones 2–8

With a varied selection of small spruces available in a variety of intriguing habits, spruces are worthy evergreens for the container garden.

Growing
Spruce trees grow best in **full sun**. The potting mix should be **neutral to acidic, moist** and **well drained**. Be sure to plant them in the biggest container you can so that they won't tip over. They should be moved to the garden after three to five years. Fertilize monthly with quarter-strength fertilizer during the growing season. Move containers to a sheltered location protected from the sun and wind in winter.

Tips
Dwarf and slow-growing spruce cultivars are used as specimens in containers. Plant them with drought-tolerant plants in mixed containers, because spruces will tend to quickly consume the available moisture.

Recommended
P. abies (Norway spruce) is a tall, upright, pyramidal tree, but it has many dwarf cultivars. '**Little Gem**' is a slow-growing, rounded cultivar. '**Nidiformis**' (nest spruce) is a slow-growing, low, compact, mounding plant. **Forma** *pendula* are variable, weeping or prostrate forms of spruce. Staked at about 1.2 m (4'), they develop into beautiful weeping specimens.

P. glauca (white spruce) is a large, pyramidal tree native to many parts of Canada. The species is too large for a container, but **var.** *albertiana* 'Conica' (dwarf Alberta spruce) is a slow-growing, dense, conical, bushy shrub. Its needles may scorch in too windy or hot a location.

Spurge
Euphorbia

E. dulcis 'Chameleon'

Spurge has bright yellow flowers that emerge early in the season. In fall its foliage turns bright shades of orange, red or purple.

Growing

Spurge grows well in **full sun** or **light shade**. The potting mix should be **humus rich, moist** and **well drained**. This plant is drought tolerant and rarely needs fertilizing. Fertilize once in the growing season, preferably just after flowering is complete, with quarter- to half-strength fertilizer. Move containers to a sheltered location protected from temperature fluctuations in winter.

Tips

Spurge is a neat, rounded plant that is well suited to low-maintenance and drought-tolerant containers.

Recommended

E. dulcis (sweet spurge) is a compact, upright plant. The spring flowers and bracts are yellow-green. The dark bronzy green leaves turn red or orange in fall. 'Chameleon' has purple-red foliage that turns darker purple in fall.

E. polychroma (*E. epithymoides*; cushion spurge) is a mounding, clump-forming plant. The inconspicuous flowers are surrounded by long-lasting, yellow bracts that give the effect of the plant being smothered in blooms. The foliage turns shades of purple, red or orange in fall. There are several cultivars, but the species is more commonly available. 'Candy' has yellow bracts and flowers, and the leaves and stems are tinged with purple.

Combine spurge with sedum and hens and chicks for a succulent mixed container.

Features: mound-forming perennial; yellow to green, spring to mid-summer flowers; decorative foliage; fall colour **Height:** 30–60 cm (12–24") **Spread:** 30–60 cm (12–24") **Hardiness:** zones 4–8

Swan River Daisy

Brachyscome (Brachycome)

B. BLUE ZEPHYR

This plant's dainty, daisy-like flowers and lacy, fern-like foliage make a winning combination.

Growing

Swan River daisy prefers **full sun** but benefits from light shade in the afternoon. The potting mix should be **well drained**. Allow the soil to dry between waterings. Fertilize once a month with half-strength fertilizer. Plant out early because cool spring weather encourages compact, sturdy growth. This plant is frost tolerant and tends to die back when summer gets too hot. If it begins to fade, cut it back and move it to a slightly shadier spot.

Tips

This versatile plant works well in mixed containers and hanging baskets. Plant it near the edges so that the bushy growth will hang out over the sides of the pot and the little flowers will poke through the leaves of any neighbouring plants.

Recommended

B. iberidifolia forms a bushy, spreading mound of feathery foliage. Blue-purple or pink-purple, daisy-like flowers are borne all summer. BLUE ZEPHYR, a Proven Winners Selection, is a more heat-tolerant cultivar that will bloom all season. **'Hot Candy'** bears heat-tolerant, dark pink flowers that fade to pale pink. **'Toucan Tango'** has heat-tolerant, mauve flowers with lime green centres.

Features: mounding or spreading habit; blue, pink, white or purple, summer flowers, usually with yellow centres; feathery foliage **Height:** 15–45 cm (6–18") **Spread:** 20–60 cm (8–24") **Hardiness:** annual

Sweet Flag
Acorus

Sweet flags have glossy, often striped leaves that create an attractive display in a mixed container of moisture-loving plants.

Growing

Sweet flags grow best in **full sun**. The potting mix should be **moist to wet**. Fertilize monthly with quarter- to half-strength fertilizer. Move containers to a sheltered location like an unheated shed or garage in winter.

Tips

These plants are much admired for their habit as well as for the wonderful, spicy fragrance of the crushed leaves. Include sweet flags in a mixed container with plants like calla lilies and elephant ears for a texturally intriguing, wet mixed container.

Recommended

A. calamus (sweet flag) is a large, clump-forming plant with long, narrow, bright green, fragrant foliage. **'Variegatus'** has vertically striped yellow, cream and green leaves.

A. gramineus (dwarf sweet flag, Japanese rush) forms low, fan-shaped clumps of fragrant, glossy, green, narrow leaves. **'Minimus Aureus'** is a very low-growing cultivar with bright golden yellow leaves. **'Ogon,'** a Proven Winners selection, has cream-and-green-striped leaves. **'Pusillus'** (dwarf Japanese rush) is a very low-growing cultivar. (Zones 5–8)

A. gramineus 'Ogon'

Sweet flag was a popular moat-side plant in the past.

Features: clump-forming perennial; narrow, stiff or arching, grass-like, sometimes variegated leaves; moisture loving **Height:** 10 cm–1.5 m (4"–5') **Spread:** 10–60 cm (4–24") **Hardiness:** zones 4–8

Thyme
Thymus

T. x citriodorus 'Golden King' with parsley, rosemary and others

In the Middle Ages, it was believed that drinking a thyme infusion would enable one to see fairies.

Features: mounding or creeping perennial; purple, pink or white, late-spring to early-summer flowers; tiny, fuzzy or glossy, often fragrant foliage **Height:** 5–45 cm (2–18") **Spread:** 10–40 cm (4–16") **Hardiness:** zones 3–8

Upright or creeping, thyme is an excellent plant for a container garden. Its tiny flowers attract a variety of pollinators.

Growing
Thyme prefers **full sun**. The potting mix should be **humus rich** and very **well drained**. Mix in compost or earthworm castings. These plants are fairly drought tolerant. Fertilize no more than monthly with quarter-strength fertilizer during the growing season. Move containers to a sheltered location protected from temperature fluctuations in winter.

Tips
Thyme grows nicely by itself or mixed with other herbs. It can also be used at the edge of a mixed container, where the tiny leaves will soften the appearance of coarser-leaved companions.

Recommended
T. **x** *citriodorus* (lemon-scented thyme) forms a tidy, rounded mound of lemon-scented foliage. The flowers are pale pink. **'Argenteus'** has silver-edged leaves. **'Aureus'** has golden yellow variegated leaves. **'Golden King'** has yellow-margined leaves. (Zones 5–8)

T. praecox subsp. *arcticus* (*T. serpyllum*; mother of thyme, wild thyme) is a low, creeping, mat-forming plant. It bears purple flowers. **'Elfin'** forms tiny, dense mounds of foliage. It rarely flowers. **'Minimus'** is lower growing than the species and bears pink flowers. **'Snowdrift'** has white flowers.

T. vulgaris (common thyme) forms a bushy mound of dark green leaves. The flowers may be purple, pink or white. **'Silver Posie'** has pale pink flowers and silver-edged leaves. (Zones 4–8)

Tradescantia

Tradescantia

Although often reserved for hanging baskets, these plants create a stunning display of arching foliage that looks lovely in a tall, urn-shaped planter.

Growing

Tradescantias grow well in **full sun** or **partial shade**. The potting mix should be **moist** and **well drained**. Fertilize every two weeks during the growing season with quarter- to half-strength fertilizer. Move containers to a sheltered location protected from temperature fluctuations in winter. Tender plants will have to be brought indoors before the first frost or replaced the following summer.

Tips

Tradescantias make good hanging-basket plants and can be grown alone or with other trailing plants. In containers they make attractive companions for coarse-textured and upright-growing plants.

Recommended

T. x *andersoniana* forms a clump of stems and arching, strap-like foliage. Clusters of blue, purple, pink, red or white flowers are produced from early summer to fall. **'Concord Grape'** has silvery blue-green foliage and dark purple flowers. **'Little Doll'** is a dwarf selection that bears light blue flowers. (Zones 3–8)

T. pallida **'Purpurea'** is a tender, trailing or mound-forming plant with purple stems and bronzy purple leaves. It bears pink flowers in summer. This plant is drought tolerant.

T. pallida '*Purpurea' is a tender perennial and must be moved indoors to a bright location if you wish to overwinter it.*

T. x *andersoniana* cultivar with hakone grass, begonia, hosta and others (above), *T.* x *andersoniana* 'Sweet Kate,' from Proven Winners (below)

Also called: silver inch plant, spiderwort
Features: clump-forming, mound-forming or trailing, hardy or tender perennial; colourful foliage; attractive, pink, blue, purple, red or white, summer flowers **Height:** 20–60 cm (8–24") **Spread:** 30–60 cm (12–24")
Hardiness: zones 3–8; grown as an annual

Tulip
Tulipa

T. hybrid

Tulips, with their beautiful, often garishly coloured, flowers are a welcome sight as we enjoy the warm days of spring.

Growing
Tulips grow best in **full sun**. The flowers tend to bend toward the light in light shade or partial shade. The potting mix should be **well drained**. Plant bulbs in fall and keep containers in a sheltered location. Bulbs that have been cold treated can be planted in spring. Fertilize with quarter-strength fertilizer every two weeks as flowering finishes and until the foliage begins to fade only if you are planning to overwinter your bulbs for blooms the next spring.

Tips
Tulips provide the best display when planted in groups in mixed or solo containers. Plant them with other spring-blooming plants for a pretty display to welcome the approaching summer.

Recommended
There are about 100 species of tulips and thousands of hybrids and cultivars. They are generally divided into 15 groups based on bloom time and flower appearance. They come in dozens of shades, with many bicoloured or multi-coloured varieties. Blue is the only shade not available. Check with your local garden centre in early fall for the best selection.

Features: perennial bulb; spring flowers
Height: 15–75 cm (6–30") **Spread:** 5–20 cm (2–8") **Hardiness:** zones 3–8

Verbena

Verbena

*V*erbena is an outstanding container and hanging-basket plant. The trailing stems poke brightly coloured flower clusters out in unexpected places.

Growing

Verbenas grow best in **full sun**. The potting mix should be very **well drained**. Fertilize every two weeks in summer with half-strength fertilizer. Pinch young plants back to encourage bushy growth.

Tips

Use verbenas in mixed containers, hanging baskets and window boxes. They are good substitutes for ivy geraniums where the sun is hot and where a roof overhang keeps these mildew-prone plants dry.

Recommended

V. x *hybrida* is a bushy plant that may be upright or spreading. It bears clusters of small flowers in shades of white, purple, blue, pink, red, salmon, coral or yellow. **Babylon Series** is a group of compact, bushy plants with flowers in shades of deep or light blue, bright or light pink, dark or light purple, red or white. **'Peaches and Cream'** is a spreading plant with flowers that open soft peachy pink and fade to white. SUPERBENA SERIES, a Proven Winners Selection, is a group of mounding then cascading, mildew-resistant plants with large, vividly coloured flowers in shades of purple, burgundy, coral, red, pink or blue.

To rejuvenate foliage and encourage more blooms, cut back the plants to half their size in mid-summer.

V. SUPERBENA DARK BLUE with salvia and spurge

Features: mounding to cascading habit; red, pink, purple, blue or white flowers, sometimes with white centres **Height:** 20–60 cm (8–24") **Spread:** 30–60 cm (12–24") **Hardiness:** tender perennial grown as an annual

Viburnum

Viburnum

V. opulus 'Nanum'

Features: bushy or spreading, evergreen, semi-evergreen or deciduous shrub; attractive, sometimes fragrant flowers; decorative, summer and fall foliage; decorative, sometimes persistent fruit
Height: 50 cm–3 m (20"–10')
Spread: 50 cm–2.4 m (20"–8')
Hardiness: zones 2–8

Good fall colour, attractive form, shade tolerance, scented flowers and attractive fruit put viburnums in a class by themselves.

Growing

Viburnums grow well in **full sun, partial shade** or **light shade**. The potting mix should be **moist** and **well drained**. Fertilize monthly with half-strength fertilizer during the growing season. Move containers to a sheltered location out of the wind and sun in winter. Move plants to the garden as they become too large to keep in containers.

Tips

Viburnums are large and shrubby and can be trained into small tree forms. Use them in large mixed planters. They are tolerant of a variety of conditions, so there are many possible companion plants to create unique combinations each year.

Recommended

Many viburnum species, hybrids and cultivars are available. A few popular ones include *V. carlesii* (Korean spice viburnum), a dense, bushy, rounded, deciduous shrub with white or pink, spicy-scented flowers (zones 5–8); *V. dentatum* (arrowwood), a shade-loving, deciduous, upright shrub with blue fruit (zones 3–8); *V. opulus* (European cranberrybush, Guelder rose), a small, rounded, spreading, deciduous shrub with lacy-looking flower clusters (zones 3–8); *V. plicatum* var. *tomentosum* (doublefile viburnum), with a graceful, horizontal branching pattern that gives the shrub a layered effect and lacy-looking, white flower clusters (zones 5–8); and *V. trilobum* (American cranberrybush, highbush cranberry), a dense, rounded shrub with clusters of white flowers followed by edible red fruit (zones 2–8).

V. plicatum var. *tomentosum* 'Mariesii' (above)
V. trilobum (below)

The edible but very tart fruits of V. opulus *and* V. trilobum *are popular for making jellies, pies and wines. They can be sweetened somewhat by freezing them or by picking them after the first frost or two.*

Vinca

Vinca

V. minor and *V. minor* 'Illumination' with geraniums

With glossy, deep green leaves and periwinkle blue flowers, vinca has an attractive presence in the container garden.

Growing

Grow vinca in **partial to full shade**. The potting mix should be evenly **moist** and **well drained**. Fertilize monthly with quarter-strength fertilizer during the growing season. Move containers to a sheltered location out of the wind in winter. This plant is evergreen and will continue to provide you with colour during the chilly, grey days of winter.

Also called: periwinkle **Features:** low, trailing, hardy or tender vine; blue-purple, pale blue, reddish purple or white, mid-spring to fall flowers; green or variegated, glossy foliage **Height:** 10–30 cm (4–12") **Spread:** 60 cm– 1.2 m (2–4') **Hardiness:** zones 3–8; tender perennial grown as an annual

Tips

Vinca is a useful, attractive filler plant for containers and hanging baskets. Poke a few rooted stems in here and there to provide a dark green background in your mixed containers.

Recommended

V. major (greater periwinkle) forms a low mat of trailing stems with glossy, dark green leaves. It bears purple or blue flowers from spring to fall. It is often grown as an annual. '**Variegata**' has irregular, creamy margins on light green, glossy leaves. (Zones 6–8)

V. minor (lesser periwinkle) forms a low, loose mat of trailing stems. A flush of purple or blue flowers is borne in spring and sporadically all summer. '**Atropurpurea**' bears reddish purple flowers. '**Sterling Silver**' has cream-edged foliage and blue flowers.

Weigela
Weigela

Weigelas have been improved through breeding, and specimens with more compact forms, longer flowering periods and greater cold tolerance are now available.

Growing
Weigelas prefer **full sun** but tolerate partial shade. The potting mix should be **well drained**. Fertilize monthly with half-strength fertilizer during the growing season. Move containers to a sheltered location protected from temperature fluctuations in winter.

Tips
With their green, bronze or purple foliage and long flowering period, weigelas can be used as focal points in mixed containers. Combine a purple-leaved weigela with a silver-leaved, white-flowered, trailing plant like snow-in-summer to soften the edges of the container and to create a lovely contrast.

Recommended
W. florida is a bushy, spreading shrub with arching branches that bears clusters of dark pink flowers. Many hybrids and cultivars are available. Some of the best selections include **'Carnival,'** with red, white or pink, thick, azalea-like flowers; MIDNIGHT WINE, a low, mounding dwarf with dark burgundy foliage; **'Polka,'** with bright pink flowers; **'Red Prince,'** with dark red flowers; **'Rubidor,'** with yellow foliage and red flowers; **'Variegata,'** with yellow-green variegated foliage and pink flowers; and WINE AND ROSES, with dark burgundy foliage and rosy pink flowers.

W. florida FINE WINE, a Proven Winners Color Choice Selection

Weigela will become too large for a container after three to five years and should be moved to the garden when it does.

Features: upright or low, spreading, deciduous shrub; attractive, late-spring, early-summer and, sporadically, fall flowers; green, bronze or purple foliage **Height:** 30 cm–1.8 m (1–6') **Spread:** 30 cm–1.2 m (1–4') **Hardiness:** zones 3–8

Yarrow

Achillea

A. millefolium

arrows are informal, tough plants with a fantastic colour range.

Growing

Yarrows grow best in **full sun**. The potting mix should be **light** and **well drained**. These plants tolerate drought. Fertilize no more than monthly with quarter-strength fertilizer. Too much fertilizer results in weak, floppy growth. Deadhead to prolong blooming. Move containers to a sheltered location protected from temperature fluctuations in winter.

Tips

Yarrow thrives in hot, dry locations where nothing else will grow. If you often forget to water, yarrow could be the plant for you. Combine it with other drought-tolerant plants like sedum and hens and chicks. The fine, ferny foliage of yarrow will contrast with the coarse, fleshy foliage of the other two plants.

Recommended

A. millefolium (common yarrow) forms a clump of soft, finely divided foliage and bears white flowers. Many cultivars exist, with flowers in a wide range of colours. '**Apple Blossom**' has light pink flowers. '**Paprika**' bears yellow-centred, red flowers that fade to pink, yellow or cream. '**Summer Pastels**' bears white, pink, yellow, purple and sometimes red or salmon-coloured flowers. '**Terra Cotta**' has orange-red flowers that fade to light rusty orange or creamy orange.

Features: clump-forming perennial; white, yellow, red, orange, pink or purple, mid-summer to early-fall flowers; attractive foliage; spreading habit **Height:** 10 cm–1.2 m (4"–4')
Spread: 30–90 cm (12–36")
Hardiness: zones 2–8

Yarrow will happily self-seed, eventually turning up in most of your containers and anywhere else the seeds happen to land.

Yew

Taxus

Yews are among the only reliable evergreens for full sun and deep shade.

Growing

Yews grow well in any light conditions from **full sun to full shade**. The potting mix should be **moist** and **well drained**. Fertilize monthly with half-strength fertilizer during the growing season. Move them to a sheltered location out of the wind and sun in winter.

Tips

Yews are often used to create topiary specimens and can be clipped to maintain a small, neat form for a container. Specimens can be planted alone or used with annuals and perennials for a mixed display.

Male and female flowers are borne on separate plants. Both must be present for the attractive, red arils (seed cups) to form.

Recommended

T. x *media* (English-Japanese yew), a cross between *T. baccata* (English yew) and *T. cuspidata* (Japanese yew), has the vigour of English yew and the cold hardiness of Japanese yew. It forms a rounded, upright tree or shrub, though the size and form can vary among the many cultivars. **'Brownii'** is a dense, rounded cultivar. **'Hicksii'** is a narrow, columnar form. **'Tautonii'** is a slow-growing, rounded, spreading cultivar.

These trees tolerate windy, dry and polluted conditions but dislike excessive heat, and on the hotter south or southwest side of a building they may suffer needle scorch.

T. x *media* 'Sunburst' (above)
T. x *media* 'Densiformis' (below)

Features: conical, columnar, bushy or spreading, evergreen tree or shrub; attractive foliage; red fruit **Height:** 30 cm–3 m (1–10') **Spread:** 30 cm–1.5 m (1–5') **Hardiness:** zones 4–7

Yucca

Yucca

Y. *filamentosa* with maidenhair vine, osteospermum, vinca and dracaena

Yucca fruits rarely develop in Canada. The yucca moth, which pollinates the flowers, is uncommon outside the plant's native range.

Also called: Adam's needle **Features:** stiff, rosette-forming, evergreen perennial; white or creamy, summer flowers; stiff, decorative foliage **Height:** 60–90 cm (24–36"); up to 1.8 m (6') in flower **Spread:** 60–90 cm (24–36") **Hardiness:** zones 5–8

ucca will add a bold presence and texture to your mixed planters.

Growing

Yucca grows best in **full sun** but tolerates partial shade. The potting mix must be **well drained**. This plant is very drought tolerant. Fertilize no more than once a month during the growing season with quarter-strength fertilizer. Move it to a sheltered location in winter, or simply leave it where it is, enjoy it covered in snow and, if it doesn't make it through winter, simply replace it in spring.

Flower spikes can be removed when flowering is finished, and dead leaves can be removed as needed.

Tips

Yucca makes a strong architectural statement and is used as a specimen in planters to give a garden a southern appearance. Combine it with low, soft, trailing plants to create some contrast.

Recommended

Y. *filamentosa* has long, stiff, finely serrated, pointed leaves with threads that peel back from the edges. It is the most frost-hardy species available. '**Bright Edge**' has leaves with yellow margins. '**Golden Sword**' has leaves with yellow centres and green margins. '**Hofer's Blue**' has attractive, blue-green leaves and is salt tolerant.

Glossary

Acidic soil: soil with a pH lower than 7.0

Annual: a plant that germinates, flowers, sets seed and dies in one growing season

Alkaline soil: soil with a pH higher than 7.0

Basal foliage: leaves that form from the crown, at the base of the plant

Bract: a modified leaf at the base of a flower or flower cluster

Corm: a bulb-like, food-storing, underground stem, resembling a bulb without scales

Crown: the part of the plant at or just below soil level where the shoots join the roots

Cultivar: a cultivated plant variety with one or more distinct differences from the species, e.g., in flower colour or disease resistance

Deadhead: to remove spent flowers to maintain a neat appearance and encourage a longer blooming season

Direct sow: to sow seeds directly in the garden

Dormancy: a period of plant inactivity, usually during winter or unfavourable conditions

Double flower: a flower with an unusually large number of petals

Espalier: a tree trained from a young age to grow on a single plane—often along a wall or fence

Genus: a category of biological classification between the species and family levels; the first word in a scientific name indicates the genus

Grafting: a type of propagation in which a stem or bud of one plant is joined onto the rootstock of another plant of a closely related species

Hardy: capable of surviving unfavourable conditions, such as cold weather or frost, without protection

Hip: the fruit of a rose, containing the seeds

Humus: decomposed or decomposing organic material in the soil

Hybrid: a plant resulting from natural or human-induced cross-breeding between varieties, species or genera

Neutral soil: soil with a pH of 7.0

Offset: a horizontal branch that forms at the base of a plant and produces new plants from buds at its tips

Panicle: a compound flower structure with groups of flowers on short stalks

Perennial: a plant that takes three or more years to complete its life cycle

pH: a measure of acidity or alkalinity; the soil pH influences availability of nutrients for plants

Rhizome: a root-like, food-storing stem that grows horizontally at or just below soil level, from which new shoots may emerge

Rootball: the root mass and surrounding soil of a plant

Seedhead: dried, inedible fruit that contains seeds; the fruiting stage of the inflourescence

Self-seeding: reproducing by means of seeds without human assistance, so that new plants constantly replace those that die

Semi-double flower: a flower with petals in two or three rings

Single flower: a flower with a single ring of typically four or five petals

Species: the fundamental unit of biological classification; the entity from which cultivars and varieties are derived

Standard: a shrub or small tree grown with an erect main stem, accomplished either through pruning and training or by grafting the plant onto a tall, straight stock

Sucker: a shoot that comes up from the root, often some distance from the plant; it can be separated to form a new plant once it develops its own roots

Tender: incapable of surviving the climatic conditions of a given region and requiring protection from frost or cold

Tuber: the thick section of a rhizome bearing nodes and buds

Variegation: foliage that has more than one colour, often patched or striped or bearing leaf margins of a different colour

Variety: a naturally occurring variant of a species

SPECIES by Common Name	LIGHT				SOIL MIX		FEATURES						
	Full Sun	Light Shade	Partial Shade	Full Shade	Soil-based	Soil-less	Variegated	Flowers	Foliage	Fruit/Seed	Scent	Specimen	Grouping
Aeonium	•	•				•			•			•	•
African Lily	•	•	•		•	•	•	•				•	•
Angel's Trumpet	•				•	•			•		•	•	•
Arborvitae	•	•	•		•				•			•	•
Argyranthemum	•					•		•					•
Asparagus Fern		•	•		•				•				•
Athyrium		•	•	•	•				•				•
Bacopa			•		•	•	•	•				•	•
Basil	•					•			•		•		•
Bay Laurel	•	•	•		•	•			•		•	•	•
Begonia		•	•					•	•				
Bidens	•					•		•	•			•	•
Black-Eyed Susan	•		•		•	•		•					•
Black-Eyed Susan Vine	•	•	•					•				•	•
Blood Grass	•		•		•	•			•	•		•	•
Blue Oat Grass	•				•	•			•	•		•	•
Bougainvillea	•					•	•	•				•	•
Bugleweed		•	•		•	•			•				•
Calla Lily	•				•		•	•	•			•	•
Canna Lily	•				•	•	•	•	•			•	•
Catch-Fly	•	•			•	•		•					•
Cilantro•Coriander	•				•	•			•		•		•
Clematis	•				•	•		•				•	•
Cleome	•				•	•		•				•	•
Clover	•	•	•		•	•			•			•	•
Coleus		•	•		•	•			•			•	•
Coral Bells		•	•		•	•		•	•				•
Cranesbill		•	•		•	•		•	•		•	•	•
Crocsmia	•				•			•	•			•	•
Cuphea	•		•			•		•					•
Dahlia	•					•		•				•	•
Daylily	•	•	•	•	•			•	•			•	•
Dogwood	•	•	•		•		•		•			•	•

	SOIL CONDITION						FORM				
Moist	Well-drained	Dry	Fertile	Average	Poor	Upright	Bushy	Climber/Trailer	Architectural	Page Number	SPECIES by Common Name
•	•			•		•			•	62	Aeonium
•	•			•		•	•			63	African Lily
•	•			•	•	•			•	65	Angel's Trumpet
•	•		•	•		•	•		•	66	Arborvitae
	•			•			•			68	Argyranthemum
•				•	•		•	•		69	Asparagus Fern
•			•	•			•			70	Athyrium
•	•			•	•			•		72	Bacopa
•	•			•	•	•	•			73	Basil
•	•			•		•	•		•	74	Bay Laurel
	•		•	•			•			75	Begonia
•	•			•	•		•	•		77	Bidens
	•			•	•	•	•			78	Black-Eyed Susan
•	•			•	•			•		80	Black-Eyed Susan Vine
•				•		•			•	81	Blood Grass
	•			•	•	•	•		•	82	Blue Oat Grass
•	•		•	•				•		83	Bougainvillea
	•			•				•		84	Bugleweed
•	•		•	•		•			•	85	Calla Lily
•	•		•	•		•			•	87	Canna Lily
•	•			•			•			88	Catch-Fly
	•	•		•	•	•	•			89	Cilantro•Coriander
•	•			•				•		90	Clematis
•	•			•	•	•			•	92	Cleome
•	•			•	•	•	•			93	Clover
•	•			•	•	•	•		•	94	Coleus
•	•		•	•			•			96	Coral Bells
	•			•	•		•			98	Cranesbill
•	•		•	•		•			•	100	Crocosmia
•	•		•	•			•			101	Cuphea
•	•		•				•			102	Dahlia
•	•			•		•			•	104	Daylily
•	•			•	•	•	•		•	106	Dogwood

SPECIES by Common Name	LIGHT				SOIL MIX		FEATURES						
	Full Sun	Light Shade	Partial Shade	Full Shade	Soil-based	Soil-less	Variegated	Flowers	Foliage	Fruit/Seed	Scent	Specimen	Grouping
Dusty Miller	•					•			•				•
Dwarf Morning Glory	•				•	•		•					•
Elder	•		•		•		•		•			•	•
Elephant Ears		•	•	•	•				•			•	•
English Ivy		•	•		•	•	•		•				•
Euonymus	•				•				•			•	•
Fan Flower	•	•			•	•		•	•				•
Fescue	•		•		•	•			•	•		•	•
Flowering Maple	•	•			•	•	•	•	•			•	•
Fothergilla	•	•	•		•			•	•		•	•	•
Fountain Grass	•				•	•			•	•		•	•
Geranium	•				•	•	•	•	•			•	•
Glory Bush	•				•	•		•	•			•	•
Hakone Grass		•	•		•	•	•		•			•	•
Hebe	•	•	•		•	•	•	•	•			•	•
Heliotrope	•				•	•		•			•		•
Hens and Chicks	•		•			•			•				•
Holly	•				•				•	•		•	•
Hosta		•	•		•		•	•	•			•	•
Hydrangea	•		•		•	•		•				•	•
Hyssop	•		•		•			•			•		•
Impatiens		•	•		•			•	•				•
Ipomoea	•					•	•		•				•
Iris	•				•		•	•	•				•
Kalanchoe		•	•			•		•	•				•
Lady's Mantle		•	•		•	•		•	•				•
Lamium		•	•		•	•	•		•			•	•
Lavender	•				•	•		•	•		•	•	•
Leymus	•				•	•			•				•
Licorice Plant	•					•			•				•
Lilac	•				•			•			•	•	•
Lilyturf		•	•		•			•	•	•			•
Lobelia	•		•		•	•			•			•	•

	SOIL CONDITION						FORM				
Moist	Well-drained	Dry	Fertile	Average	Poor	Upright	Bushy	Climber/Trailer	Architectural	Page Number	SPECIES by Common Name
	•	•		•	•		•			108	Dusty Miller
	•			•	•		•			109	Dwarf Morning Glory
•	•			•	•	•	•		•	110	Elder
•			•	•		•			•	112	Elephant Ears
•	•		•	•	•		•	•		113	English Ivy
•	•			•	•					114	Euonymus
•	•			•	•		•	•		116	Fan Flower
•	•			•	•		•		•	117	Fescue
•	•			•		•	•			118	Flowering Maple
•	•			•	•	•	•		•	119	Fothergilla
	•			•	•	•			•	120	Fountain Grass
	•	•		•	•	•	•	•		122	Geranium
•	•			•		•	•			124	Glory Bush
•	•			•			•		•	125	Hakone Grass
•	•			•			•			126	Hebe
•	•		•	•			•			127	Heliotrope
	•			•	•		•	•		128	Hens and Chicks
•			•			•	•		•	129	Holly
•	•			•			•		•	131	Hosta
•	•		•			•	•		•	133	Hydrangea
	•			•		•	•			135	Hyssop
•	•			•			•			136	Impatiens
	•			•	•		•	•	•	137	Ipomoea
•	•			•	•	•			•	139	Iris
	•			•	•		•		•	141	Kalanchoe
•	•		•				•			142	Lady's Mantle
•	•			•	•		•	•		143	Lamium
	•			•	•	•	•		•	145	Lavender
•	•			•	•	•	•		•	146	Leymus
	•			•	•		•	•		147	Licorice Plant
	•		•	•	•	•	•		•	148	Lilac
•	•		•	•		•			•	150	Lilyturf
•	•		•	•		•	•	•		151	Lobelia

SPECIES
by Common Name

SPECIES by Common Name	LIGHT				SOIL MIX		FEATURES						
	Full Sun	Light Shade	Partial Shade	Full Shade	Soil-based	Soil-less	Variegated	Flowers	Foliage	Fruit/Seed	Scent	Specimen	Grouping
Lotus Vine	•	•	•		•	•			•				•
Lungwort			•	•	•		•	•	•				•
Lysimachia	•				•			•	•				•
Magnolia	•		•		•				•		•	•	•
Maidenhair Fern		•	•		•				•				•
Maple	•	•			•				•			•	•
Marguerite Daisy	•				•			•					•
Million Bells	•					•		•				•	•
Mondo Grass		•	•		•	•		•	•			•	•
Monkey Flower		•	•		•	•		•					•
Nasturtium	•				•	•	•	•	•				•
Nemesia	•					•		•				•	•
Nicotiana	•	•	•		•	•		•			•		•
Oregano	•				•	•			•		•		•
Osteospermum	•					•		•				•	•
Oxalis	•				•	•		•	•				•
Pansy	•				•	•		•					•
Parsley	•		•		•	•			•				•
Penstemon	•				•			•					•
Perilla	•		•		•	•			•			•	•
Persicaria	•		•		•			•					•
Petunia	•					•		•				•	•
Phormium	•				•	•			•			•	•
Piggyback Plant		•	•	•	•		•		•			•	•
Plectranthus		•	•		•	•	•		•		•	•	•
Rose	•				•	•		•			•	•	•
Rosemary	•				•	•			•		•	•	•
Rush	•		•		•		•		•			•	•
Salvia	•				•	•		•	•		•		•
Scarlet Runner Bean	•				•	•	•	•	•			•	•
Sedge	•		•		•	•			•	•		•	•
Sedum	•					•	•	•	•				•
Serviceberry	•	•			•				•		•	•	•

Moist	Well-drained	Dry	Fertile	Average	Poor	Upright	Bushy	Climber/Trailer	Architectural	Page Number	SPECIES by Common Name
	•			•	•		•	•		153	Lotus Vine
•	•		•				•			154	Lungwort
•	•			•	•	•		•	•	155	Lysimachia
•	•		•			•	•		•	156	Magnolia
•	•		•	•	•		•		•	158	Maidenhair Fern
	•		•	•		•	•		•	159	Maple
	•			•			•			161	Marguerite Daisy
•	•			•			•	•		162	Million Bells
•	•			•	•		•		•	163	Mondo Grass
•			•				•			164	Monkey Grass
•				•	•		•	•		165	Nasturtium
•	•		•	•			•	•		166	Nemesia
•	•			•		•			•	167	Nicotiana
	•			•	•		•	•		168	Oregano
•	•		•	•		•	•			169	Osteospermum
	•			•			•	•		170	Oxalis
•	•			•	•	•				171	Pansy
•	•		•	•	•		•			173	Parsley
	•			•			•			174	Penstemon
•	•			•	•	•	•		•	175	Perilla
•	•		•	•		•	•			176	Persicaria
•	•			•	•	•	•	•		177	Petunia
•	•			•	•	•			•	178	Phormium
	•			•			•	•		179	Piggyback Plant
•	•			•	•		•	•		180	Plectranthus
•	•		•	•		•	•		•	181	Rose
•	•			•	•	•	•			183	Rosemary
•			•	•		•			•	184	Rush
•			•			•	•			185	Salvia
•	•			•	•		•	•		187	Scarlet Runner Bean
•	•	•		•		•	•		•	188	Sedge
	•			•	•	•	•	•		190	Sedum
•	•			•		•	•		•	191	Serviceberry

SPECIES
by Common Name

Species	Full Sun	Light Shade	Partial Shade	Full Shade	Soil-based	Soil-less	Variegated	Flowers	Foliage	Fruit/Seed	Scent	Specimen	Grouping
Snapdragon	•				•	•		•					•
Snow-in-Summer	•		•		•	•		•	•				•
Spider Plant			•	•		•	•		•				•
Spruce	•				•				•			•	
Spurge	•	•			•	•		•	•				•
Swan River Daisy	•					•		•				•	•
Sweet Flag	•				•		•		•	•		•	•
Thyme	•				•	•	•		•		•		•
Tradescantia	•	•	•		•	•		•	•				•
Tulip	•				•	•	•	•					•
Verbena	•				•			•				•	•
Viburnum	•	•	•		•			•	•	•		•	•
Vinca			•	•	•	•	•	•	•				•
Weigela	•				•			•	•	•		•	•
Yarrow	•				•	•		•	•				•
Yew	•	•	•	•	•				•			•	•
Yucca	•				•	•			•			•	•

Moist	Well-drained	Dry	Fertile	Average	Poor	Upright	Bushy	Climber/Trailer	Architectural	Page Number	SPECIES by Common Name
	•		•	•		•	•			192	Snapdragon
	•			•	•		•	•		194	Snow-in-Summer
•	•			•	•		•	•	•	195	Spider Plant
•	•			•	•	•	•		•	196	Spruce
•	•			•			•	•		197	Spurge
	•	•	•	•			•	•		198	Swan River Daisy
•				•	•	•	•		•	199	Sweet Flag
	•		•	•	•		•	•		200	Thyme
•	•		•	•		•	•	•		201	Tradescantia
	•		•	•	•	•			•	202	Tulip
	•			•			•	•		203	Verbena
•	•			•	•	•	•		•	204	Viburnum
•	•		•	•	•			•		206	Vinca
	•			•		•	•		•	207	Weigela
	•			•	•	•	•			208	Yarrow
•	•			•	•	•	•		•	209	Yew
	•	•		•	•	•			•	210	Yucca

Index of Recommended Plant Names

Main entries are in **boldface**; botanical names are in *italics*.

African Lily

Bacopa

Coleus

Salvia

Tradescantia

Weigela

Ju ly

About the Authors

Laura Peters is a certified Master Gardener with 23 gardening books to her credit. She has gained valuable experience in every aspect of the horticultural industry in a career that has spanned more than 18 years. She enjoys sharing her practical knowledge of organic gardening, plant varieties and gardening products with fellow gardeners.

I would like to thank my parents, Gary and Lucy Peters, for their love and support. I would also like to thank my fellow Lone Piners for their incredibly hard work and for coming together as a team to complete this project, but a super big thanks to Don Williamson, Alison Beck, Sheila Quinlan and Heather Markham. Thanks to Proven Winners for the use of their beautiful images and to everyone who allowed us to photograph their innovative, fun and unique containers, from coast to coast. Lastly I'd like to acknowledge everyone who has shared their knowledge of container gardening with me over the span of my gardening life and career. Every lesson was valuable and useful, and I hope that our readers are able to use this book for their own container gardening adventures.

Alison Beck is a professional garden writer who has been gardening since she was a child. Author of over two dozen books on gardening, her writing showcases her talent for practical advice and her passion for gardening. Alison has a diploma in Horticultural Technology as well as a degree in Creative Writing from York University.

I would like to thank my family, friends and co-workers for their support and hard work, especially Robin who helped me through the long days of writing.

Veteran garden writer **Don Williamson** is the co-author of several popular gardening guides. He has a degree in Horticultural Technology and extensive experience in the design and construction of annual and perennial beds in formal landscape settings.

Don thanks the Creator.